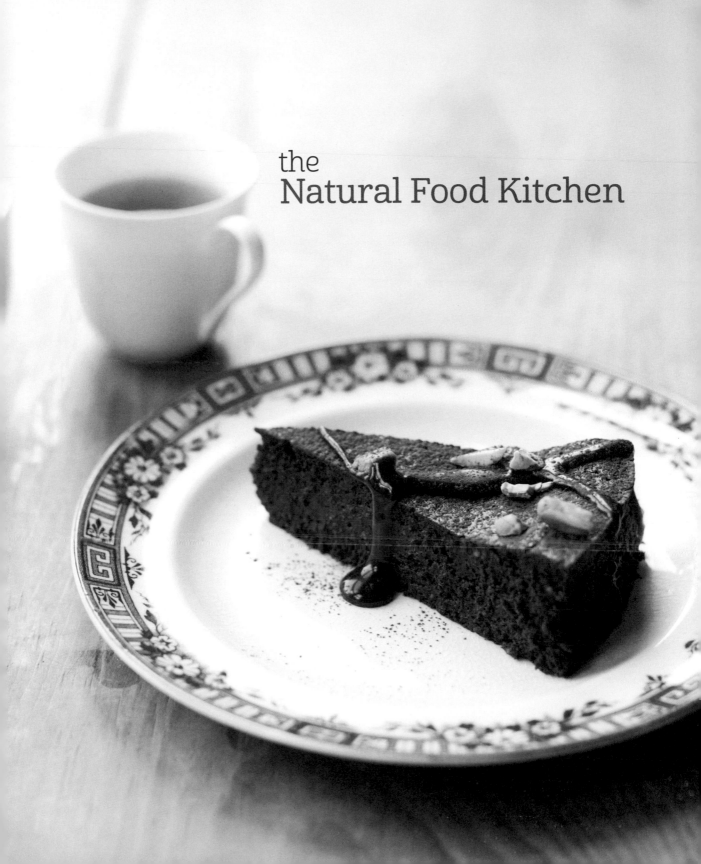

the
Natural Food Kitchen

the Natural Food Kitchen

delicious, globally inspired recipes using
only the best natural and seasonal produce

Jordan Bourke

photography by Tara Fisher

RYLAND PETERS & SMALL
LONDON • NEW YORK

Designers Maria Lee-Warren
and Megan Smith
Photography Art Direction
Megan Smith
Commissioning Editor Nathan Joyce
Production Manager Gordana
Simakovic
Art Director Leslie Harrington
Editorial Director Julia Charles

Food Stylist Jordan Bourke
Prop Stylist Jo Harris

First published in 2014
by Ryland Peters & Small
20–21 Jockey's Fields,
London WC1R 4BW
and
519 Broadway, 5th Floor,
New York NY 10012

www.rylandpeters.com

10 9 8 7 6 5 4 3 2 1

ISBN: 978-1-84975-560-3

Printed and bound in China

A CIP record for this book is available
from the British Library.

US Library of Congress Cataloging-
in-Publication Data has been applied
for.

Notes

• All spoon measurements are level,
unless otherwise specified.

• Ovens should be preheated to the
specified temperature. Recipes in this
book were tested using a regular
oven. If using a fan-assisted/
convection oven, follow the
manufacturer's instructions for
adjusting temperatures.

• All eggs are medium (UK) or large
(US), unless otherwise specified.
It is recommended that free-range,
organic eggs be used whenever
possible. Recipes containing raw or
partially cooked egg, or raw fish or
shellfish, should not be served to the
very young, very old, anyone with
a compromised immune system or
pregnant women.

• When a recipe calls for the grated
zest of citrus fruit, buy unwaxed fruit
and wash well before use. If you can
only find treated fruit, scrub well in
warm soapy water and rinse before
using.

• Please note: This is not an allergy
cookbook, and the recipes are not
strictly free from sugar, wheat/gluten
or dairy. If you suffer from allergies or
intolerances you should seek out
alternative products and professional
advice, if needed. Neither the
authors nor the publisher can be held
responsible for any claim arising out
of the information in this book.
Always consult your health advisor or
doctor if you have any concerns
about your health or nutrition.

Contents

Introduction

Food is more than just fuel for your body and mind, but one of life's most enjoyable and sensual experiences. So, with these objectives in mind, I have gathered together some of my favourite globally inspired dishes, which will not just feed your body and mind, but also your heart and soul.

How to cook naturally

There was a time when the mere mention of eating healthy natural foods would generate moans and groans, as people presumed that virtuous eating meant bland, boring and tasteless foods. Those days are long gone, as this generation is better educated and more widely travelled, and fully aware of the fact that *we are what we eat.*

I have a huge appetite, so I don't believe in abstinence or denial. I do like knowing what is in my food though, and eating a diet that is, as much as possible, free from refined and overly processed ingredients. I also find that my general health is greatly improved when I cook with alternatives to refined wheat, cane sugar and dairy. Having suffered in my teens and early twenties with various little ailments from migraines to non-stop colds, I soon realised they were all directly linked to what I was eating, and when I cut back on these ingredients, everything about my health improved. I had more energy, fewer coughs and colds, my migraines disappeared, I slept better... the list goes on.

Of course, as luck would have it, many of my favourite dishes were made with cane sugar, refined wheat and dairy, so, not wanting to resign myself to a life of deprivation, I put my chef's hat on and set about recreating the recipes using some alternative ingredients. At the time, most of my friends thought I was a lunatic and regarded things like 'rice milk' with extreme caution, but I persevered, and now, 10 years later with myself and my sister's first cookbook 'The Guilt-Free Gourmet' a great success, it seems people's appetites are really changing. The great news is, it's now very easy to get your hands on the ingredients that were once hard to come by, with everything from spelt flour to coconut oil stocked in all the major supermarkets, as well as health food stores that are popping up all over the place.

Many of you may be thinking, 'surely wheat and dairy products are completely natural anyway?', and yes, some of them are. What you need to watch out for are the products that have been mass-produced and highly processed, with preservatives added in to suit long shelf-life requirements. Refined white wheat and dairy are also the foods that 90 % of the people I cook for have issues with and are trying to cut down on, so it made sense to offer alternatives for these ingredients in my recipes.

Unfortunately, even products sold as health foods can be misleading, so as a general rule, I would encourage you to read the ingredients of whatever product you are buying, regardless of how natural and healthy it professes itself to be, and avoid products with chemical sounding ingredients that you have never heard of. Where possible, it's also worth considering buying organic, as the number of pesticides, fungicides, and antibiotics they contain is significantly less than non-organic.

With all of my recipes I have tried to be as exact as possible, but I always encourage the use of one's senses and intuition – it will make you a better cook in the long run. I am not suggesting you fling the recipes out the window and approach the dish with gleeful abandon; there are measurements and cooking times for a reason. However, they will sometimes need to be adjusted depending on the cooking conditions and also the ingredients themselves. For example, the temperature of home ovens are a law unto themselves and cause chaos with baking recipes. I recently checked one of my client's swanky new ovens using an oven thermometer, and it's a good 20°C (40°F) hotter than the marked temperature! So if you find your cake is almost cooked on the outside and decidedly uncooked on the inside, trust your instincts, cover it with foil, turn down the temperature and increase the cooking time, checking as you go. Follow your taste buds and gut instinct, as well as the recipe.

Pantry essentials

While the seasons hold the most sway over me in terms of what and how I cook, it is my pantry of dry goods that I turn to to bring these fresh ingredients alive. Below are the pantry essentials used in this book. Obviously you do not need to go out and buy the lot in one go, just slowly build it up as you cook the dishes that appeal to you most. The vast majority of these ingredients have long shelf-lives, so you can come back to them as and when you please.

If there is one thing I use a lot of, it is **olive oil**. I use a fairly standard, inexpensive extra virgin olive oil for frying and roasting, and then for drizzling and salad dressings I have a few more special extra virgin olive oils, with more grassy and peppery notes. I also make sure never to heat or cook with the more special oils as it ruins their flavour, not to mention their nutritional profile. I also use **organic sunflower oil** for any shallow or deep-frying and **chilli oil** for a bit of heat. I use a lot of **virgin coconut oil**, but you'll find more about that in the dairy alternatives section. **Vinegars** are the perfect counter to good olive oil and the ones I use most are **red wine, sherry** and good quality **balsamic vinegar** from Modena, which is far more viscous and sweeter then the other two.

When I want to season something with salt, there are a number of ways to achieve this, with quite different results. I use good quality **sea salt** and **Himalayan pink salts** most – they have much better flavour then table salt and have not been stripped of all their nutrients and minerals. In curries and Asian dishes, I mainly use good Vietnamese **fish sauce** and Korean **soy sauce**, and there are plenty other good-quality brands available in supermarkets. For coeliacs/celiacs, gluten-free **tamari** soy sauce is a good option, but it is strong, so I usually water it down a little.

For sweet treats and baking, **vanilla extract**, **rose** and **orange blossom water** give cakes a real lift. If you need to set something, **agar flakes** can be used instead of **gelatine** if you are vegetarian.

I cook a lot with **noodles** as they are so versatile – my favourites are **rice vermicelli** and flat **rice/stick noodles**; these are the ones that you would have come across if you have eaten in a Vietnamese restaurant – they also happen to be gluten-free. **Soba** are thin and robust with a slightly nutty flavour, usually made with a mix of buckwheat (which is actually wheat-free) and wheat flour, but you can also find some that are made from 100 % buckwheat. **Udon** are wheat-based noodles, thick, round and springy; flat rice noodles are a good wheat-free alternative.

When it comes to bulking up a dish, I turn to **grains**, **beans** and **pulses**. They do need a bit of love flavour-wise, but once you get that right they really do sing. **Chickpeas** and **borlotti** beans are so versatile and a great source of protein, but the dried variety do need soaking overnight. **Lentils**, whether **green**, **red**, **puy** or **beluga** all cook reasonably quickly, just remember to season them when still warm so they absorb all the flavours.

Rice is a staple around the world, but there are so many different varieties, tastes and textures. My favourites are **jasmine**, **brown short-grain**, **camargue**, and **carnaroli**, all of which are used in this book. My other staples are **quinoa**, the mighty seed, which has become extremely popular now, but still divides people with its texture, and also **farro** (see page 94).

I use a lot of **Asian ingredients** as well, and most of them you will be able to find in a supermarket, although you'll find more choice and often better flavour profiles in specialist Asian food stores. This is particularly true for roast **sesame seed oil**, the Asian brands being far superior to the western supermarket versions. **Mirin** is a slightly sweet, low alcohol rice wine that has a really distinctive flavour. My favourite brand is Clearspring **mikawa mirin** as it is made the traditional way with no added sugar or glucose syrup. Japanese **miso paste** (made with fermented soy beans) is easy to find; the Korean version known as **doenjang** has a deeper, more powerful flavour, but my all time favourite is **gochujang** – a Korean spicy chilli paste. All of these pastes often have added corn syrup, so try to find the more natural brands. For a hit of sourness, **tamarind** is a must. I buy mine either fresh in a pod like fruit, or in a paste, which is a lot more convenient and easy to use; again read the ingredients and look for 100% tamarind. Japanese **dashi stock** is made from kombu (kelp) and shaved, fermented **bonito fish flakes**, but you can also buy it in a dried format in Asian markets.

I use a lot of **nuts** and **seeds**. Whether sprinkled into porridge, blitzed into the base of a tart or used to thicken a sauce, they are extremely versatile and provide great depth of flavour. If you open my cupboard, you will always find **almonds**, **pecans**, **hazelnuts**, **cashews**, **walnuts**, **pistachios**, **pine nuts**, **sunflower seeds**, **pumpkin seeds** and **sesame seeds**.

Spices provide the backbone of flavour for so many dishes, my cooking and recipes would be lost without them. I won't single out any here as they all have an important place in my cooking. When it comes to buying them, look for reasonably small quantities, so you can use them up within a few months, when they are still fresh and at their best.

Alternatives to sugar

Added sugars have received a lot of negative press recently and have been directly linked to an increase in type-2 diabetes and various other diet- related illnesses. Cane and beet sugar and high fructose corn syrup (HFCS) are the worst offenders, added into a shocking amount of pre-packaged foods that you would not expect to contain sugar, resulting in the estimated 20 teaspoons of added sugar consumed per day by the average person in the UK. Sadly, many people see all sugars, whether added or natural, in the same light. I have spoken to a surprisingly large number of people in recent months who have started cutting whole fruit out of their diet in their quest to reduce their sugar intake, not realizing that eating an apple is not the same as eating a spoon of cane sugar. It's important to remember that naturally occurring sugars in fruit and vegetables are needed by our bodies for energy. Wherever there is sugar in nature, there is also fibre, and this slows down the rate of absorption of sugar into our blood, so you don't get the blood sugar level peaks that you would get with sugar on its own. As long as you aren't eating 20 bananas a day, fresh fruit and vegetables are fine and should not be cut from your diet.

There are now an ever-increasing number of sugar alternatives, all marketing themselves as natural and healthy. The reality is that all added sugars, even the less refined, less processed alternatives, still need to be eaten in moderation, regardless of what it says on the label. Personally I try to keep the amount of added sugar I consume to a minimum, and I never use cane or beet sugar or golden syrup. I do love desserts though, and there are times in life when you want to be able to indulge, so in these instances, and in a lot of the dessert recipes in this book, I use organic pure **maple syrup** and **coconut palm sugar**. While they are certainly far less processed and refined, and have not had vitamins and minerals stripped away, like with white cane and beet sugar, they are still an added sugar, so the old adage 'everything in moderation' still stands. Where I need to use a pale coloured sugar, I use **xylitol**. Yes it does have a horrible chemical-sounding name, but it does not belong to the class of artificial sweeteners that have recently received bad press. It's a sweetener that the body recognises as natural because it is present in all plant cells and is derived from tree bark and corn husks. It has a very low impact on blood sugar levels and it doesn't feed mouth bacteria, so it's better for dental health. It does go through a fair amount of processing though, so I use it sparingly.

At the time of writing my last book, I had also been using raw organic **agave syrup**. However, a number of reports have emerged in recent years that suggest it is highly refined and processed in a manner akin to the production of HFCS. So until it is proven otherwise I use organic pure maple syrup.

Probably the most natural way to sweeten a dish is with fruit, so I use **Medjool dates** and dried fruit, blitzed up into dishes to lend a subtle sweetness.

Alternatives to dairy

Dairy tends to divide people. There are those who love all dairy products and don't experience any physical problems digesting them. And then there are those, like me, who, for whatever reason, are mildly intolerant to it. It does strike me as odd though that human beings are the only animal that consumes dairy after weaning, and are also the only animal that consumes dairy from another species than our own. In any case, each to their own – if you feel great consuming dairy, knock yourself out. If, however you are like me and feel less then fantastic if you consume a lot of it, then there are plenty of wonderful alternatives.

Chief among them is the **coconut**. I adore coconuts! In this book I use **coconut milk** to make everything from ice cream and curry to rice pudding, soups and pancakes. It is incredibly versatile, has a subtle flavour and a lovely texture. **Coconut butte**r or **oil** are one and the same, the former is just the solidified version, which you are more likely to have come across if you live in colder parts of the world. In fact, I usually mark the beginning of my summer when it is finally warm enough for my coconut butter to melt to oil. It also has a number of health benefits, including very strong anti-microbial and anti-viral properties, and it contains lauric acid, which has anti-oxidant properties that help improve the texture of the skin and hair. There are now also a number of brands of coconut yogurt that are delicious. If you can't get your hands on that, you could try organic non-GM **soya yogurt**, which is widely available.

Rice, oat and **nut milks** are also becoming increasingly popular, but avoid brands with added sugar and buy organic where possible. **Sunflower spread** is a good alternative to butter in baking, just make sure it is made with non-hydrogenated vegetable oils and sustainably sourced palm oil.

Alternatives to wheat

Wheat is another one of these ingredients that people love to hate these days. I believe that the increasing number of allergies and intolerances that are surfacing have more to do with the production methods used to make these products, rather than the wheat itself, mass-produced white sliced bread being a perfect example. A number of people I have cooked for were convinced they had a wheat intolerance based on their body's negative reaction to mass-produced bread. In fact, most of them were reacting badly to the additives and chemicals added to these products to achieve consistent baking performance and perfect looking bread that is permanently soft. When they stopped eating these products and instead ate freshly baked bread from a bakery, made with nothing more then flour, water, yeast and salt, they felt absolutely fine and all their symptoms went away. The quality of the wheat used for the flour is also important, as for mass-produced goods, it is often bred for its high yield, stripped of its nutrients and bleached. So, with any flour, wheat or otherwise, look for ones that are 100 % natural with no additives, and preferably organic.

Of course, there are people who truly do have an intolerance, and for those that are not coeliac/celiac, I encourage them to try **spelt flour**. Spelt is often confused as being the same as wheat, however while they are related, they are two different species (spelt is triticum spelta and wheat is triticum aestivum). Spelt does contain a small amount of gluten, so it is not suitable for coeliacs/celiacs, but for those with a mild intolerance to wheat, many people find they have no problem tolerating spelt.

I also use flours like **rice, chickpea** and **cornflour/cornstarch**, which lend recipes a certain flavour profile or act as a thickener. **Oats** and **oatcakes/oat biscuits** are also useful for tart bases and crumbles.

Small Bites

All of these dishes are great for sharing. From the light and fresh Avocado Miso Dip with Root Vegetable Crisps, to the more robust and full of flavour Imam Bayildi (stewed aromatic aubergine/eggplant). Perfect for any time of the day, really!

This smooth guacamole with a Japanese twist is so quick and easy to make and another great use for miso paste. As avocado discolours quickly, be sure to make this dip just before serving. Dukkah, an Egyptian nut and spice mix, is delicious served with olive oil and bread or vegetables for dipping, but you can also sprinkle it over soups and in salads. It keeps very well if covered tightly.

avocado miso dip
with root vegetable crisps and dukkah spice mix

20 g/2½ tablespoons blanched hazelnuts

20 g/2½ tablespoons blanched almonds

2 tablespoon sesame seeds

1 tablespoon cumin seeds

1 tablespoon coriander seeds

1 tablespoon dried mint

120 g/4 oz. avocado

1 tablespoon brown miso paste

1 tablespoon freshly squeezed lemon juice

2 teaspoons tahini

2 teaspoons extra virgin olive oil

1 small garlic clove, crushed

sea salt

For the root vegetable crisps/chips:

2 medium beet(root)

2 medium parsnips

sea salt

mandolin grater

Serves 2

You can buy a packet of root vegetable crisps/chips if you're pushed for time, but if you'd like to make your own, first preheat the oven to 200°C (400°F) Gas 6. Peel, top and tail 2 beet(root) and 2 parsnips (or any other root vegetable), then using a mandolin grater, cut into paper-thin slices. Pat dry with paper towels. Place in a bowl and toss lightly with olive oil to give them a very thin coat, too much and they will be soggy rather then crisp. Toss with a little sea salt then lay out one-by-one and not overlapping on 2 oven trays lined with parchment paper. Roast for 5–8 minutes, keeping a sharp eye on them as they burn easily. Remove and leave to cool completely before moving them to a bowl.

Reduce the oven temperature to 180°C (350°F) Gas 4.

Roast the nuts and seeds on separate trays, the hazelnuts for about 5 minutes and the almonds for about 8 minutes. Leave to cool.

Meanwhile, in a dry frying pan/skillet over a medium heat, fry the cumin seeds and coriander seeds for 1–2 minutes until fragrant.

In a food processor, blitz the spices, roasted nuts, seeds, dried mint and ¼ teaspoon of sea salt until finely ground. Be careful not to blend for too long, though, as the nuts will begin to release oils and it will turn from a powder to a paste. Carefully spoon the mixture into a bowl and set aside.

Blitz the avocado in the food processor with the miso paste, lemon juice, tahini, olive oil and garlic until completely smooth. Taste and adjust the seasoning if necessary.

Serve the vegetable crisps/chips in a shallow serving bowl.

Scatter some of the dukkah onto the avocado miso dip and drizzle with oil. To eat, dunk the crisps/chips into the dip and then into the remaining dukkah, which will cling nicely onto the wet dip.

I rarely remember famous quotes, but there is one that has managed to lodge itself somewhere in my head: 'Simplicity is the ultimate sophistication.' It was Leonardo Da Vinci who uttered these words originally, perhaps not about food, and yes, it is a little pompous, but when I heard it, the first thing I thought of was cooking. With the odd exception, I really believe this statement to be true. Keep it simple. This is one such dish, a small celebration of three new season spring vegetables – asparagus, peas and broad/fava beans.

pea, broad bean & mint purée
with asparagus, soft-boiled egg and chilli flakes

extra virgin olive oil
½ an onion (about 70 g/3½ oz.), finely chopped
200 g/1⅓ cups shelled broad/fava beans
200 g/1⅓ cups shelled fresh peas
2 eggs
1 garlic clove, crushed
1 small handful fresh mint leaves
1 unwaxed lemon, zested
sea salt
300 g/10 oz. fine asparagus, woody ends broken off
freshly ground black pepper
½ teaspoon dried chilli/hot red pepper flakes

Serves 4

Place a frying pan/skillet over a medium heat with 1 tablespoon of olive oil, add in the chopped onion and sauté for 10 minutes until translucent, making sure not to let them colour. Keep to one side.

Bring a large saucepan of water to the boil. Add in the broad/fava beans, one minute later add in the peas, leave both to boil for a further 3 minutes, then remove the beans and peas to a bowl of ice-cold water, reserving the pan of boiling water.

Gently lower the eggs into the boiling water. Turn down the heat a little and simmer the eggs for 6 minutes exactly, then remove from the pot (reserving boiling water again) and plunge the eggs into cold water.

While the eggs are cooking, remove the outer skin from the broad/fava beans. Drain the peas and beans and add to a food processor with the onion, garlic, mint, lemon zest, 2 tablespoons of olive oil and ¾ teaspoon sea salt. Pulse a few times on and off, scraping down the sides, until combined. I like it with a little bit of bite, so I don't completely blitz the peas and broad/fava beans, but it's up to you. Adjust the seasoning with salt, pepper and a little more olive oil if necessary.

After you have removed the eggs, add 1 teaspoon of salt to the boiling water and add in the asparagus. Boil for 2–3 minutes, depending on their thickness, until just tender, with a little bite. Place the asparagus into cold water to stop them cooking, remove and drain.

To serve, carefully remove the shell from the soft-boiled eggs. Spoon some of the purée onto a plate, top with some asparagus spears and a quarter of an egg, then sprinkle over some dried chilli/hot red pepper flakes and drizzle over a little more olive oil. Serve immediately.

Imam bayildi is the original Turkish name for this dish; literally meaning the imam (priest) fainted. The story goes the imam was either so overcome by the superb taste of his wife's dish or horrified by the quantity and cost of olive oil she used, that he fainted! In fact, this dish is neither expensive or over-indulgent in its use of oil. Nevertheless, it's still worth using good quality extra virgin olive oil.

imam bayildi
(stewed aromatic aubergines)

3 medium
  aubergines/eggplants
sea salt
2 onions, about 245 g/
  ½ lb., thinly sliced
5 garlic cloves, crushed
2 teaspoons coconut
  palm sugar
1 teaspoon
  smoked/Spanish
  paprika
300 g/10 oz. baby plum
  or cherry tomatoes,
  finely chopped
1 large handful fresh
  flat-leaf parsley, finely
  chopped, plus extra
  to garnish
freshly ground black
  pepper
100 ml/scant ½ cup
  extra virgin olive oil
juice of ½ a lemon

Serves 3–4

Rinse the aubergines/eggplants. Keeping the stalks on, peel off 4–5 vertical 2 cm/¾ inch strips of skin, from top to bottom, leaving a space between each peel so you are left with strips of skin and exposed flesh around the aubergine/eggplant. Make a vertical cut right through the centre, from top to bottom, but leave both ends intact, so the 2 halves hold together. Sprinkle plenty of salt over the exposed areas of flesh and inside the vertical cut and leave in a colander with a weighted plate on top to drain out some of the bitter juices.

Meanwhile make the filling. In a frying pan/skillet, gently sweat out the sliced onion with a splash of oil over a medium heat until soft and translucent. Take care not to colour them. Add in the garlic, coconut palm sugar and smoked/Spanish paprika and cook for another couple of minutes, without burning the garlic. Stir in the chopped tomatoes and the chopped parsley. Season with salt and pepper and remove from heat.

Rinse the salt off the aubergines/eggplants, gently squeezing out any excess liquid and pat dry. Lay the aubergines/eggplants in a medium size pot that will just fit them snugly, divide all the tomato mixture between them, gently and carefully stuffing it into the incision so as not to pull the 2 halves apart. Cover with the olive oil, lemon juice and enough water to submerge about ¾ of the aubergines/eggplants. Add in a good pinch of salt and pepper and place on a medium-high heat. Once bubbling, reduce the heat to low and leave to barely simmer for 1 hour with the lid on, until the aubergines/eggplants are completely soft. You may need to turn them once half way through. Taste the sauce and adjust seasoning if necessary. Leave to cool.

Serve at room temperature with the extra parsley sprinkled over and plenty of spelt bread, sourdough or focaccia (see page 49) to mop up the liquid. The flavour of this dish is even better the following day, so it is a great one to make in advance.

Simple and quick, these are perfect for a light lunch, or as a casual appetizer. You can also experiment a little, by adding in or substituting your favourite herbs or spices. Corn and little chunks of chorizo are a delicious alternative to the chickpeas.

pan-fried chickpea fritters

2 teaspoons cumin seeds
½ teaspoon dried chilli/ hot red pepper flakes
250 g/1 cup soy or Greek yogurt
1 tablespoon pure maple syrup
sea salt
120 g/1 cup spelt flour (white or wholegrain)
½ teaspoon baking powder
170 ml/¾ cup rice, soy or dairy milk
1 egg, lightly beaten
400-g/14-oz. can chickpeas, drained and rinsed
100 g/1 small red onion, finely chopped
1 small handful fresh flat-leaf parsley, finely chopped
1 small handful coriander/cilantro, finely chopped
olive or vegetable oil, for frying
1 spring onion/scallion, finely sliced diagonally
extra virgin olive oil, for drizzling

Makes 16

In a dry frying pan/skillet, gently fry the cumin seeds over a medium heat until aromatic. Pound ½ of them to a powder using a pestle and mortar, and keep the other ½ to one side. In a bowl, combine together the ground cumin, chilli/hot red pepper flakes, yogurt, maple syrup and a good pinch of sea salt. Set to one side.

Place the flour and baking powder in a large bowl, slowly whisk in the rice, soy or dairy milk and beaten egg, until well combined with no lumps. Add in the chickpeas, red onion, almost all of the herbs, remaining cumin seeds, ¾ teaspoon sea salt and a few grindings of black pepper. Stir together to combine.

Place 1 tablespoon of olive or vegetable oil in a large, non-stick frying pan/skillet and set over a medium-high heat. Once hot, add 2 level tablespoons of batter for each fritter and flatten into little rounds. Fry in batches, without overcrowding the frying pan/skillet, for about 5 minutes, turning once, until they are golden brown and cooked through.

To serve, pile the fritters up on individual plates and scatter over the sliced spring onions/scallions and extra parsley. Serve with a green salad. Finally, drizzle over some extra virgin olive oil. Spoon the set-aside yogurt mixture over the top or serve it in a bowl on the side.

Beet(root) is in season right through the winter months and into January when its earthy, clean flavour is wonderful for people who want to be a little more virtuous, but don't want to miss out on flavour. This salad is a great all rounder, filling enough to be served on its own for brunch, or it could also work as a small appetizer.

beetroot, cherry tomatoes & soft-boiled eggs on rye bread

300 g/10 oz. large beet(root), topped, tailed and cut into 2 cm/³⁄₄ in. wedges (skin-on)

2 teaspoons olive oil

300 g/10 oz. new potatoes (I like the red-skinned roseval variety)

3 eggs

½ small red onion, thinly sliced

2 tablespoons extra virgin olive oil, plus more to serve

1 teaspoon wholegrain mustard

sea salt and freshly ground black pepper

4 slices rye bread, cut lengthways

1 garlic clove, peeled and halved

handful of rocket/arugula

12 cherry tomatoes, halved

1 spring onion/scallion, finely sliced

Serves 4

Preheat the oven to 180°C (360°F) Gas 4. In a roasting tray, toss the beet(root) wedges with the olive oil and season. Roast for 30–35 minutes or until tender and the skins are beginning to blister. Turn the oven off, but leave the beet(root) in to keep warm.

In a saucepan, cover the potatoes generously with cold, salted water. Bring to the boil and simmer briskly for 10 minutes. Add the eggs to the pan and simmer for another 6–7 minutes. Remove the eggs with a slotted spoon and plunge into ice-cold water. Cook the potatoes for a further few minutes until tender. Drain, then roughly cut in half while still warm. Combine the potatoes with the red onion, 1 tablespoon of extra virgin olive oil and the wholegrain mustard; season and set aside.

Toast the bread and while still hot rub generously with the cut side of the garlic, almost grating it against the rough surface of the toasted bread. Divide the toasted rye bread between plates and then drizzle over another tablespoon olive oil and sprinkle with sea salt.

Place a few leaves of rocket/arugula on top of the toast, then tumble over some potatoes, beet(root) and tomatoes. Finish with the soft-boiled eggs, peeled and cut into wedges and the spring onions/scallions, scattered over. Season again, if needed and drizzle over a little more extra virgin olive oil. Serve immediately.

This was one of the first dishes I tried after getting off the plane in Tokyo, and I've been cooking it ever since. This thick and moist cabbage-based pancake is a great dinner party dish to make with friends, frying them up one at a time and adding different toppings. Originally from Osaka, the name means 'grill as you like it', so you really can make it your own.

Okonomiyaki

100 g/¾ cup white spelt flour

¼ teaspoon baking powder

½ teaspoon sea salt

150 ml/⅔ cup instant dashi stock, or fish or vegetable stock

2 eggs

300 g/10 oz. cabbage – cut into fine strips

3 spring onions/scallions, finely chopped diagonally, reserve some for plating

2 tablespoons vegetable oil

100 g/3½ oz. raw prawns/shrimp

2 tablespoons kewpie (Japanese mayonnaise, see tip right), or normal mayonnaise

2 tablespoons Okonomiyaki sauce (see tip, right)

2 tablespoons bonito flakes – (dried, smoked tuna flakes, see right)

1 tablespoon pickled sushi ginger

Serves 2

In a large bowl combine the flour, baking powder and salt. Whisk in the dashi (or fish or vegetable stock) and eggs. Then add in the cabbage and most of the spring onions/scallions and combine together.

In a non-stick frying pan/skillet add in a tablespoon of the vegetable oil and heat over a medium-high heat. Add in ½ the batter in a neat round shape about 15 cm/6 inches in diameter; don't flatten it out, as Okonomiyaki should be thick. Place half the prawns/shrimp on top so they sit into the batter, cover the pan with a fitted lid and cook for about 3–4 minutes until the bottom is set and golden. Carefully turn over, place the lid back on and cook for a further 3–4 minutes until the prawns/shrimp are cooked through and the surface is golden. Turn over one last time and cook for a further 2 minutes with the lid off.

Slide the pancake onto a plate drizzle over half of the kewpie or mayonnaise and the Okonomiyaki sauce, and then top with the bonito

flakes and remaining spring onions/scallions. Serve immediately with the pickled ginger on the side. Repeat for the second pancake.

TIP: You can buy Okonomiyaki sauce (as well as kewpie mayonnaise, dashi stock and bonito flakes) in an Asian market, or online. The Okonomiyaki sauce contains a small amount of sugar cane, so if you are trying to avoid this, you can replace it with a homemade sauce, made by mixing 1 tablespoon of soy sauce and 1 teaspoon of rice vinegar. It will be too thin to drizzle on top, so serve it as a dipping sauce on the side.

One of the reasons I have always gravitated towards the food of the Orient is because, by its very nature, it is naturally healthy, yet full of flavour. This Vietnamese pancake is a perfect example, made with rice flour and coconut milk.

Vietnamese crispy pancake
with nuoc cham dipping sauce

For the nuoc cham dipping sauce:
2 garlic cloves, very finely chopped
2 bird's eye chillies/chiles, very finely chopped
2 tablespoons rice vinegar
1 tablespoon freshly squeezed lime juice
3 tablespoons fish sauce (see tip below)
2 tablespoons maple syrup
110 ml/scant $\frac{1}{2}$ cup water

For the filling:
250–300 g/8–10 oz. cooked prawns/shrimp
200 g/2 cups beansprouts
bunch of fresh mint
large lettuce leaves
spring onions/scallions, sliced into 7.5-cm/ 3-inch lengths

For the pancake batter:
220 g/1$\frac{3}{4}$ cups rice flour
1 tablespoon cornflour/cornstarch
1 teaspoon ground turmeric
1 teaspoon coconut palm sugar
sea salt and freshly ground black pepper
a 400-ml/14-oz. can coconut milk
300 ml/1$\frac{1}{4}$ cups cold water

Makes 8

For the nuoc cham sauce, combine together the garlic, chilli, rice wine vinegar and lime juice in a small bowl and leave for 5 minutes. Add in the rest of the ingredients, mix well and leave to one side.

To make the batter, sift both flours and turmeric into a large bowl. Stir in the coconut palm sugar, and a pinch of salt and pepper. Slowly whisk in the coconut milk and water, ensuring there are no lumps.

Place a large 22–24-cm/8$\frac{1}{2}$–9$\frac{1}{2}$-inch non-stick frying pan/skillet over a high heat. Add a teaspoon of vegetable oil, and once smoking hot, ladle in a thin layer of the batter, swirling around to evenly cover the base of the pan. Turn the heat down to medium-high and fry for 3 minutes, then add on some beansprouts and prawns/shrimp and cook for a further 2 minutes. The bottom of the pancake should be crisp and golden. When it is, fold over the pancake and slide it off onto a plate. It is best when just cooked, so I like to serve them immediately one at a time. Start cooking another one when you are nearly finished eating the first. To eat, create a parcel with a large lettuce leaf, add in a good chunk of the pancake, beansprouts, prawns/shrimp and some mint, wrap it up tightly and dunk in the dipping sauce with each bite.

TIP: For the 'nuoc cham', use a good-quality Vietnamese fish sauce. Look out for the word 'nhi' on the label, which means the liquid has come from the first extraction from the fish.

This light salad is just one example of the many things you can do with gravlax, the Scandinavian home-cured fish. The assembly is quick and easy, it's just the 2-day curing time that puts people off. Once you've made the effort, though, it then lasts for at least 10 days if well-wrapped in the fridge, ready to brighten up just about any dish. I have used beet(root) here, not only for the stunning colour clash, but also for its earthy flavour. This is also a fantastic make-ahead recipe, you just assemble everything at the last moment to wow your guests!

beetroot-cured salmon (gravlax)
with an orange and celery salad

1 side of salmon, about 750 g/1½ lbs, skin on, scaled and boned

120 g/generous ½ cup sea salt

3 tablespoons xylitol

350 g/12½ oz. raw beet(root), peeled and coarsely grated

1 teaspoon freshly ground black pepper

30 g/⅓ cup fresh dill leaves

1 orange, zested, then peeled and segmented

zest of 2 unwaxed lemons

½ stick/rib celery, very thinly sliced diagonally

sea salt and freshly ground black pepper

extra virgin olive oil

handful of lamb's lettuce/mâche or rocket/arugula

1 tablespoon fresh flat-leaf parsley, roughly chopped

Serves 2 as a salad (the salmon alone serves 8–10)

For the salmon, rub your finger along the flesh to check for any pin bones, and remove with tweezers.

In a bowl combine together the salt, xylitol, grated beet(root), black pepper, dill, orange zest and the zest of 1 lemon.

Place a large sheet of clingfilm/plastic wrap inside a baking sheet (one with sides, not completely flat). Lay the side of salmon on top, skin-side down. Cover the flesh with the beet(root) mix, then very tightly wrap the clingfilm/plastic wrap around the salmon, and then wrap it with a further 2 sheets of clingfilm/plastic wrap. Place a weighted tray on top of the salmon and leave to cure in the fridge for 48 hours.

After 48 hours, pour away any juices, remove the clingfilm/plastic wrap and scrape off the beet(root) mix with your hands until clean. Thinly slice as much of the cured salmon as you want.

For the salad, season the celery with a little salt, pepper and a drizzle of olive oil and combine with the lamb's lettuce/mâche or rocket/arugula and parsley. Plate up with the segmented orange and strips of cured salmon, with a little more olive oil drizzled over.

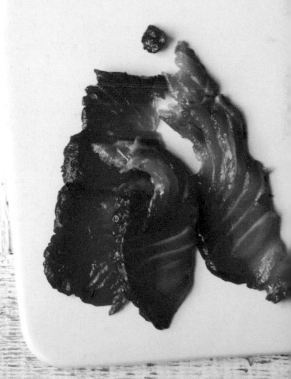

Squid is easy to cook once you know how. It either has to be cooked over a very high heat for just a couple of minutes (or it will become tough), or long and slow over a low heat, until meltingly tender. Here, the squid is briefly fried until crisp on the outside and served with a Moorish almond, chilli and lime zest crumble that you take a little of with each mouthful. For a satisfying crunch, I find that adding a little semolina to the flour mix before frying does wonders. It is not essential if you don't have it, though, and remember that semolina is not wheat-free.

crispy squid salad
with almonds, chilli & lime crumble

100 g/²⁄₃ cup whole almonds

2 tablespoons coconut palm sugar

grated zest of 1 lime

1 garlic clove, peeled and finely chopped

1 fresh red chilli/chile, deseeded and finely chopped

small handful fresh flat-leaf parsley, finely chopped

500 g/1 lb. cleaned squid (ask your fishmonger to prepare it for you)

vegetable oil, for frying

60 g/¹⁄₂ cup white spelt flour

60 g/¹⁄₂ cup semolina (optional)

sea salt and freshly ground black pepper

large handful lamb's lettuce/mâche or rocket/arugula

Serves 4

Preheat the oven to 180°C (360°F) Gas 4.

Roast the almonds for 8 minutes and leave to cool. Then, add them to a food processor and pulse on and off until they resemble coarse breadcrumbs, before removing them to a bowl. Add the coconut palm sugar, lime zest, finely chopped garlic (don't crush or mince as you want it to retain their shape), chilli/chile, parsley and 1 teaspoon of ground sea salt. Mix thoroughly and set aside.

Rinse the squid and pat dry. Then cut the body of the squid into rings and diamond shapes and cut the tentacles in half.

Pour about 5 cm/2 inches of vegetable oil into a medium saucepan, just enough to cover the squid. Place over a medium heat until a piece of bread dropped into the oil browns in about 40 seconds. Add the flour and semolina (if using) into a bowl and season well with salt and pepper. Dredge the squid in the flour mixture until well coated. Add the squid into the pan in batches, cooking for 3–4 minutes until they are a pale golden colour and crisp. Make sure you do not overcrowd the pan as it will bring down the temperature of the oil, resulting in soggy and rubbery squid. Remove the squid from the pan with a slotted spoon to drain off the oil and keep warm while you fry off the rest. Work quickly here, as you don't want the first batch sitting around.

Plate up the squid with the salad leaves mixed through, sprinkle over a little of the almond mix and serve the rest on the side. The best way to eat this is to take a little of the almond mix, then top with the squid and devour in one go. A spoon is the best implement for this, as it prevents any of the almond and spice mix from escaping!

Soups & Sandwiches

Soups and sandwiches are the ultimate comfort food, and I love how different they can be when you travel abroad. Spain's Ajo Blanco, a chilled almond and olive oil soup, is in stark contrast with the hearty Moroccan Harira, while Denmark's beautiful Smørrebrød is like the sophisticated cousin of Italy's more rustic, yet altogether sumptuous focaccia. And all are equally delicious.

This is one of those simple, comforting and totally delicious Japanese noodle soups that I find myself making all the time. If I am pushed for time I don't even bother leaving the tofu for half an hour, simply marinading it briefly before frying. Good-quality Japanese udon noodles are available in most supermarkets; they are made with wheat flour, so if you are avoiding wheat, use rice noodles instead.

udon noodle soup
with crispy tofu

½ block firm tofu (about 200 g/6½ oz.), drained

5 tablespoons tamari or dark soy sauce (or gluten-free tamari if coeliac/celiac)

3 tablespoons mirin

2 tablespoons coconut palm sugar

sea salt

200 g/6½ oz. mange tout/snow peas

400 g/14 oz. udon noodles or rice noodles

1.5 litres/quarts dashi stock from powder (see page 12), or fish or vegetable stock

5-cm/2-inch piece of ginger, peeled and cut into chunks

sunflower oil

2 spring onions/scallions, sliced

sesame seeds, to serve

Serves 4

Wrap the drained tofu in a clean dish towel and very gently squeeze to remove excess water. Remove the dish towel and slice into 16 pieces of equal size.

In a wide bowl, combine together the tamari or dark soy sauce, mirin and coconut palm sugar. Add in the tofu, cover with the marinade and leave to infuse for 25 minutes.

Bring a pot of salted water to the boil, add in the mange tout/snow peas and cook for 2 minutes, then remove (reserving the water for the udon) and plunge into cold water. Cook the udon noodles according to the packet instructions, then rinse under running cold water.

Remove the tofu from the marinade (reserve the marinade) and shake off any excess. Add the dashi and ginger to a small saucepan, almost bring to a boil and add in the reserved tofu marinade, then reduce the heat to a gentle simmer.

Place a frying pan/skillet over a medium-high heat, and add in 1 tablespoon of sunflower oil. When hot, add in the tofu and fry for 1 minute on each side until golden. Remove, drain and keep warm.

When ready to serve, add the udon and mange tout/snow peas to the stock until warmed through, then immediately ladle into bowls (avoiding the ginger), top with the tofu, spring onions/scallions and sesame seeds and serve.

Vietnamese pho (pronounced fuh) is one of these incredibly satisfying south East Asian dishes that somehow manage to be rich and full of flavour, whilst at the same time being beautifully light and fragrant.

Vietnamese pho

2 onions, quartered,
   no need to peel
100 g/3½ oz. fresh
   ginger, halved
3 garlic cloves, unpeeled
2 teaspoons whole black
   peppercorns
2 sticks cinnamon
7 star anise
6 whole cloves
1 black cardamom pod
   (optional)
1½ tablespoons
   coriander seeds
1 kg/2¼ lbs. beef bones,
   half with marrow
2½ tablespoons fish
   sauce
2 tablespoons coconut
   palm sugar
1 tablespoon freshly
   squeezed lime juice
375 g/13 oz. flat rice
   noodles
150 g/5 oz. beef fillet,
   very thinly sliced
100 g/1 cup beansprouts
3 spring onions/scallions,
   sliced on the diagonal
1 small handful each of
   fresh coriander/
   cilantro and mint (Thai
   basil optional extra)
2 limes, cut into wedges
2 fresh red chillies/chiles,
   sliced

Serves 4

Place a dry frying pan/skillet on a high heat, and when extremely hot add in the onion, ginger and garlic. Stir-fry for a few minutes until a little charred. Remove and leave to cool, then peel them and remove any burnt areas. Place the spices in the same dry pan/skillet and set over a medium heat for a few minutes until aromatic.

Place the beef bones in a large pot of cold water and bring to a boil for 5 minutes, discard the water, rinse the bones and the pot, then return them to the pot together with the ginger, onion, garlic, spices and 3 litres/quarts water, enough to generously cover the bones. Bring to a boil, reduce the heat and simmer with the lid off for 2½–3 hours until the liquid has reduced by a third. Strain the broth through a muslin-/cheesecloth-lined sieve/strainer and return the liquid to the pot. Add in the fish sauce, coconut palm sugar and lime juice. Taste and adjust the seasoning with more if necessary.

Cook the rice noodles according to the package instructions, then plunge into cold water and separate to stop them from sticking. When ready to serve, bring the broth to a rolling boil, distribute the noodles into bowls topped with the sliced raw beef. While the broth is bubbling, ladle it into the bowls so it poaches the beef and warms the noodles.

Serve immediately and scatter the beansprouts, spring onions/scallions, herbs, limes and chillies/chiles.

SHORT CUT: I also make this without the bones using beef stock instead. Simply add 2 litres/quarts of beef stock to a pot with the ginger, onion and all the spices. Bring to a boil and then simmer for about 45–60 minutes to reduce. Then follow the rest of the recipe.

Normally I would say Harira is ideal for cold winter days – hearty and warming, full of lentils, chickpeas and aromatic herbs and spices. However, the first time I tasted it was in the ferocious summer heat of Fez in Morocco, where during Ramadan, it is traditionally served in the evening to break the fast. Despite the heat, I remember adoring the vibrant and nourishing flavours of this soup, so I suppose you can enjoy it at any time of the year.

Moroccan harira soup

1 large onion, chopped
2 celery stalks, finely chopped
1 carrot, peeled and chopped into 1-cm/³⁄₈-inch pieces
2 fresh red chillies, deseeded and finely chopped
4 garlic cloves, peeled and crushed
1 tablespoon cumin seeds
2 teaspoons ground turmeric
2 teaspoons smoked/Spanish paprika
2 teaspoons ground cinnamon
2-cm/³⁄₄-inch piece of fresh ginger, peeled and finely grated
a good pinch of saffron fronds/threads (optional)
3 bay leaves
450 g/1 lb. lamb, cut into 1-cm/¹⁄₂-inch pieces
3 tablespoons tomato purée/paste
1.2 litres/quarts chicken or vegetable stock
2 x 400-g/14-oz. cans chopped tomatoes
400-g/14-oz. can chickpeas, drained and rinsed
150 g/³⁄₄ cup brown or green lentils
a bunch of fresh coriander/cilantro, chopped
a bunch of flat-leaf parsley, chopped
sea salt and freshly ground black pepper
extra virgin olive oil
1 lemon, cut into wedges to serve

Serves 4–6

Heat 3 tablespoons of the oil in a large, heavy-based saucepan set over a medium heat. Add in the onion, celery, carrot and chillies, and cook until the onions have softened. Add in the garlic, all the spices and bay leaves and cook for another 2 minutes, stirring all the time. Add in the lamb and tomato purée and cook for another couple of minutes, then add in the stock and canned tomatoes. Bring to the boil, reduce the heat and simmer very gently with the lid on for 45 minutes.

Remove the lid, add the chickpeas and lentils and cook for another 20–30 minutes, or until the lentils are cooked.

Season the soup with salt and pepper. If you have used stock cubes, you will only need a small amount of extra salt; however, if you have used home-made stock with no added salt, you will need to add about 2 teaspoons of sea salt, and stir in most of the chopped coriander/cilantro and parsley.

Ladle into deep bowls, drizzle over a little extra virgin olive oil, sprinkle with the remaining herbs and serve with the lemon wedges to squeeze over. A hunk of sourdough bread alongside would not be a bad idea, either.

Originating in Andalucía, the hot and arid part of southern Spain, it is perhaps no surprise that this elegant almond and garlic soup is served ice-cold. Growing up, I spent a lot of time in Spain as we have great family friends there; I have a vivid memory of arriving at a small town called Écija in an area near Seville nicknamed the 'frying pan' because it is so hot. We were foolish enough to visit in July, when it very much lived up to its nickname and had to seek refuge in the first restaurant we came upon. Small and dimly lit, as the shutters had been pulled closed to keep out the sun, the thick walls kept the inside blissfully still and cool. We had no choice in what we were given to eat, but we were not disappointed and the cooling ajo blanco was the star of the show. They served theirs with muscat grapes, but I think I prefer it with melon. The choice is yours. Either way, this ice-cold soup (you can even serve it with ice cubes if you wish) is perfect on a summer's day. For the uninitiated, it may sound unusual, but trust me, it is delicious.

ajo blanco with melon

200 g/1⅓ oz. whole almonds, skin on

50 g/2 oz. day-old bread, spelt or sourdough, crusts removed

3 small garlic cloves, peeled

sea salt

250 ml/1 cup good-quality extra virgin olive oil, plus extra to serve

420 ml/1½ cups ice-cold water

2 tablespoons sherry vinegar

1 melon, cantaloupe or charentais, cut into 4-cm/1½-inch wedges

Serves 4–6

Cover the almonds with boiling water. Leave for 5 minutes, then one-by-one, pinch the almonds, squeezing them out of their skins (you can buy blanched almonds, but I find that the method I suggest improves the taste).

Place on a dry frying pan/skillet over a medium heat for a couple of minutes. You don't want to toast the almonds, just dry them out and tickle out their flavour with a bit of heat.

Add to a food processor with the bread, garlic and 2 level teaspoons of sea salt and blitz until very fine. When it is almost a paste, while still blitzing, drizzle in the olive oil very slowly until it is thick and smooth. Then slowly pour in the water and red wine vinegar. Taste and adjust the seasoning if necessary with a little more vinegar, salt or olive oil. Refrigerate for at least 2 hours until thoroughly chilled.

Taste again prior to serving, as the flavours will change slightly as they get to know each other in the fridge. The soup will also thicken as it cools, so you can add in a few tablespoons of water if you want to thin it out a little. Ladle into chilled bowls and top with the wedges of melon. Drizzle over a little more extra virgin olive oil and serve immediately.

I love how the sleek and stylish Danes even manage to make an open faced sandwich appear almost like a modern art installation. Elegant and refined, yet not at all lacking in flavour, these beautiful slices of rye bread topped with an assortment of ingredients make a great lunch, or if you make them smaller they could be lovely canapés.

smørrebrød
Danish open-faced rye sandwiches

½ a red onion, very thinly sliced

1 tablespoon red wine vinegar

3 new potatoes

3 tablespoons mayonnaise (see page 106), or good-quality store-bought

4 slices of rye bread

½ an avocado, peeled and stoned/pitted

sea salt and freshly ground black pepper

small handful of cress

2 baby pickled gherkins, thinly sliced

1 radish, thinly sliced

1 teaspoon chives, finely chopped

2 asparagus spears

100 g/3½ oz. sliced smoked salmon

small handful of fresh dill fronds/threads

Makes 4

Place the sliced red onion in a bowl and combine with the red wine vinegar. Leave to pickle and colour for at least 30 minutes.

Put the new potatoes in a saucepan of lightly salted water and bring to the boil. Simmer until just tender, about 10 minutes depending on size. A sharp knife should glide in without much resistance. Drain and leave to cool.

Spread a thin layer of mayonnaise on the 4 slices of rye bread, leaving the rest aside. Slice the potatoes and avocados into 1-cm/⅜-in thick slices. Top 2 of the rye bread slices with layers of potato and avocado and sprinkle over a little salt and pepper. Spoon some of the remaining mayonnaise across the centre of each slice of bread, then position the cress on top of the line of mayonnaise. Arrange a few slices of gherkin on top and scatter over some of the red onion slices and radish slices. Finally sprinkle over the chives.

For the other 2 slices of rye bread, first, using a peeler, shave the asparagus spears lengthways, so you have thin ribbons of asparagus. Position the salmon onto the bread and spoon the remaining mayonnaise on top. Curl the shaved asparagus with your fingers and place on top, and finally finish with some dill fronds/threads. Season with a sprinkle of sea salt and black pepper and serve immediately.

TIP: as there are small quantities of asparagus, avocado, new potatoes, radish, gherkins, red onion and herbs used in this recipe, you can use any remaining ingredients to make a killer salad. Just cook the potatoes and combine together with the onion, mayonnaise, avocado, gherkins, radish, herbs, shaved asparagus, salmon and a glug of good olive oil. Season to taste.

Warm focaccia, drowned in grassy extra virgin olive oil and topped with an array of beautiful Italian antipasti, this is the stuff of lazy lunches – everything on the table and all your family and friends gathered around dipping in. I love the very subtle nutty flavour that comes through with spelt flour and it works really well in bread and pasta recipes. It has become popular of late for its lower gluten content, which means almost no kneading, as well as it being easier to digest.

rosemary spelt focaccia
with Italian antipasti

For the focaccia:
500 g/4 cups white spelt flour
2 teaspoons sea salt, plus extra for sprinkling
1 x 7 g sachet fast-action yeast
400 ml/1²⁄₃ cups warm water
3 tablespoons olive oil, plus extra for drizzling
1 teaspoon pure maple syrup
8–10 cherry tomatoes, halved
16–20 rosemary sprigs
sea salt

Antipasti suggestions:
sun-dried tomatoes
olives
artichokes
figs
rocket/arugula
pesto
roasted red (bell) peppers
Parma or serrano ham
extra virgin olive oil

Serves 4–6

For the focaccia, sift the flour into a large bowl and stir in the salt (if using salt flakes, crush it between your fingers so it is fine) and yeast, ensuring everything is well mixed together. Make a well in the centre and add in the warm water, olive oil and maple syrup all at once and bring together with a wooden spoon to form a wet and sticky dough. Cover the bowl with clingfilm/plastic wrap and leave in a warm place (beside a switched-on oven or a radiator) to rise for 30 minutes.

Once the dough has risen a little, cover one hand with a little olive oil to prevent sticking, then pull the edges of the dough away from the side of the bowl, pick it up completely and firmly slap it back down into the bowl. Pick up the side of the dough and fold it over on itself, turning the bowl a quarter turn at a time. Repeat this process for 2 minutes, using a little more oil to prevent sticking if necessary. Cover the bowl again and leave for about 1 hour (in a warm place again) or until it has almost doubled in size.

Generously oil a baking sheet, pull the dough out of the bowl onto the tray and press it into a rough oblong shape. Leave to rise for a final 45–60 minutes (again in a warm place) until almost doubled in size again.

Preheat the oven to 200°C (400°F) Gas 6. When the dough has risen again, use your fingertips to firmly dimple the dough in 16–20 places, adding a little sprig of rosemary to each dimple. Dot the halved tomatoes around the surface. Lightly drizzle over a little olive oil and sprinkle over some sea salt, then bake for 20–25 minutes, or until golden. To check it is cooked, turn the focaccia on its side and tap the bottom – it should sound hollow.

Leave to cool for long enough that it doesn't burn your hand when tearing into it, and serve warm with your favourite selection of antipasti from the list to the left, or indeed anything else that takes your fancy.

My wife and I are big falafel fans. The smell of them cooking, the crunchy exterior, the aromatic spices, and of course the beautiful emerald green centre from all the chopped herbs. Stuffed into a pitta or wrap, slathered in creamy houmous and spicy sambal – there's nothing like it. After sampling pretty much every falafel restaurant and van in London, I started making our own. Apart from the time it takes to soak the beans (overnight), they are quick and easy to make at home and perfect for a lazy Sunday or a casual meal with family and friends. If you can't get the broad/fava beans, you can also make these falafel with just chickpeas.

falafel wrap
with houmous and sambal dressing

250 g/1¼ cups dried chickpeas, soaked overnight

200 g/1 generous cup fresh shelled broad/fava beans, or dried split broad/fava beans, soaked overnight

5 garlic cloves, peeled

1 small red onion, peeled and roughly chopped

big handful coriander/cilantro, leaves only

big handful flat-leaf parsley, leaves only

¼ teaspoon cardamom, pounded, or ground cardamom

1 teaspoon ground cumin

1 teaspoon smoked/Spanish paprika

½ teaspoon baking powder

1 teaspoon sea salt

sunflower or other vegetable oil, for frying

houmous, to serve

sambal or other chilli/chile paste, to serve (some chilli/chile pastes contain refined cane sugar, so check the ingredients if you are avoiding it)

pitta bread or wraps, spelt- or gluten-free, if required

cherry tomatoes, to serve

rocket/arugula, to serve

Makes 4–5 wraps

Drain the chickpeas (and the broad/fava beans, if you are using dried). In batches, add them into a food processor together with the garlic, red onion, herbs, spices, baking powder and salt. Blitz until everything is finely chopped and very well combined. Using your hands, firmly press the mixture into slightly flattened small golf-ball shapes. Place on a tray and refrigerate for 30 minutes.

Pour 2.5 cm/1 inch of vegetable oil into a medium size frying pan/skillet and set over a medium-high heat. Test the heat by adding in a piece of bread or a very small piece of the falafel mixture – it should brown in about 40–50 seconds when ready. Add the falafel in batches, but don't overcrowd the pan as it will bring the temperature down. Fry for a couple of minutes on each side until golden brown on the outside. Remove and drain on paper towels. Keep warm while you cook off the rest of them.

Toast a pitta bread or warm a wrap in the oven, spread with a generous amount of houmous and as much of the spice paste as you like. Add in 4–5 falafel with some rocket/arugula and halved cherry tomatoes. Tightly wrap it up and eat immediately with some extra houmous and sambal on the side.

Salads &
Lighter Dishes

Gone are the days of limp lettuce, anaemic tomatoes and nail-varnish remover for dressing. Salads are now the voluptuous and abundant star of the show. Juicy, fresh fruit and vegetables, hearty grains and pulses and vibrant herbs and spices combine to create a dish that is as far from a supporting act, as Marilyn Monroe in *Some Like it Hot*.

Tuscans beware, this isn't a classic panzanella. I can see traditionalists everywhere with eyes rolled up to heaven and lips pursing, but I don't care, I love this incarnation of the original dish. The mellow sweetness of the grilled peaches works perfectly with the crunchy bread and olive oil. I have also made it with nectarines – good if you have an aversion to the furry coat of peaches – and you can add rocket/arugula or other leaves if you want more greens in your salad, but this is the place to start.

peach panzanella

½ small red onion, very thinly sliced

½ tablespoon red wine vinegar

2 peaches, stoned/pitted and cut into 2-cm/¾-inch wedges

15 baby plum tomatoes, halved

1 avocado, stoned/pitted, skinned and chopped into bite-size chunks

1 full-length slice of sourdough bread

1 small garlic clove, halved

2 tablespoons extra virgin olive oil

a bunch of basil, roughly chopped

1 teaspoon Thai red chilli/chile paste

sea salt and freshly ground black pepper

Serves 2

Place the sliced red onion in a bowl with the red wine vinegar and a pinch of sea salt. Toss together and set aside to allow the flavours to infuse.

Place a grill pan over a high heat. Lightly brush the peach wedges with just enough olive oil to coat them. Add the peaches to the pan and cook for a couple of minutes until charred on one side. Flip over and cook on the other side. Transfer to a plate while you prepare the other ingredients.

In a large mixing bowl gently toss the chopped tomatoes and avocado chunks together with the cooked peaches in 1 tablespoon of extra virgin olive oil and a good pinch of salt. Set aside.

Toast the sliced sourdough bread until golden brown and crunchy on the outside. Rub the garlic clove over the hot bread, then drizzle some olive oil over the bread and leave it to soak in.

Finely chop the leftover garlic and add it to the tomato mix, together with the chopped basil and vinegar-infused red onion slices.

For the dressing, combine the Thai red chilli/chile paste with the remaining tablespoon of the extra virgin olive oil in a small bowl. Add this into the salad bowl and then tear the bread into the salad in rough chunks. Gently combine everything together until well mixed. Taste and season with a grinding of black pepper and more sea salt if needed.

Pile the panzanella onto a flat serving dish and serve immediately.

Apparently this salad, which has its origins in the Sichuan region of China, got its name from the sound of street traders pounding the cooked chicken in order to shred it. It is such a crowd pleaser – perfect for picnics and BBQs as you can keep the sauce separate until everyone is ready to eat.

bang bang chicken salad

500 ml/2 cups chicken stock

30 g/1 oz. ginger, peeled and chopped

1 teaspoon Sichuan or black peppercorns

2 star anise

450 g/1 lb. skinless chicken breasts

100 g/3½ oz. pak choi/bok choy leaves, finely sliced

1 large carrot, peeled and julienned or grated

1 small cucumber, halved and deseeded

4 spring onions/scallions, cut into thin strips

handful fresh coriander/ cilantro leaves

2 limes, cut into wedges

For the sauce:

150 g /⅔ cup almond or peanut butter (crunchy)

1 tablespoon sesame seed oil

1 tablespoon soy sauce

1 fresh red chilli/chile, deseeded, finely sliced

1 tablespoon pure maple syrup

1 tablespoon rice wine vinegar

1 small garlic clove, peeled and crushed

½ teaspoon finely grated ginger

Serves 4–6

Place the stock, ginger, peppercorns, star anise and 1 teaspoon salt in a pot and bring to a boil. Add in the chicken, reduce heat a little and simmer for 10 minutes until cooked through. Leave to cool for 20 minutes, then remove the chicken, drain and leave to cool completely. Reserve 120 ml/½ cup of the cooking liquid and discard the rest. When the chicken is cold shred it with your hands, or slice very finely.

In a bowl combine together all the sauce ingredients (apart from the red chilli/chile) and slowly mix in the reserved cooking liquid a tablespoon at a time until you have a sauce the consistency of pouring cream.

Peel the cucumber halves into long thin strips and cut into 7.5-cm/ 3-inch lengths. Combine together the pak choi/bok choy, carrot, cucumber, spring onions/scallions, shredded chicken, most of the coriander/ cilantro leaves and the sauce. Serve in a large dish with the remaining coriander/cilantro leaves and red chilli/chile on top and the limes on the side to squeeze over.

This light noodle salad uses a nuoc cham sauce that is similar to the Vietnamese pancake recipe on page 30; some of the herbs are the same too, so I often cook these dishes on consecutive days to make the best use of the ingredients. For a vegetarian version try it with tofu fried in vegetable oil until crisp and golden.

bun xao
(rice noodle salad with herbs)

400 g/14 oz. sirloin/New York strip steak, sliced into thin strips

2 tablespoons fish sauce

1 garlic clove, crushed

1 stalk lemongrass, outer leaves removed and finely chopped

225 g/8 oz. rice vermicelli noodles

1 tablespoon vegetable oil

1/2 a red onion, halved and thinly sliced

150 g/5 1/2 oz. cucumber, halved and thinly sliced

1 medium carrot, peeled and julienned or coarsely grated

handful of fresh mint and coriander/cilantro leaves, Thai basil (optional), plus extra to serve

2 tablespoons roasted cashews, plus extra to serve

2 limes, cut into wedges

For the nuoc cham sauce:

2 garlic cloves, peeled and very finely chopped

1 bird's eye chilli/chile, very finely chopped

3 1/2 tablespoons rice vinegar

2 tablespoons freshly squeezed lime juice

3 1/2 tablespoons fish sauce

2 tablespoons pure maple syrup

3 tablespoons water

Serves 4

Make the nuoc cham sauce by combining together the garlic, chilli/chile, rice wine vinegar and lime juice and leave for 5 minutes. Add in the rest of the ingredients, mix well and set aside.

In a bowl, combine together the sliced steak (without the fat) with the fish sauce, garlic and lemongrass and set aside.

Cook the noodles according to the packet instructions, which usually involves covering them with boiling water for about 6 minutes to soften, then rinsing with cold water and draining.

Heat a frying pan/skillet over a high heat, add in the vegetable oil and when extremely hot add the steak. Stir-fry for a few minutes until cooked through. Remove and leave to one side.

In a large bowl combine together the noodles, red onion, cucumber, carrot, beef, herbs, nuts and the sauce. Thoroughly mix together and serve in bowls with the lime wedges and remaining herbs and nuts sprinkled on top.

It is not perhaps the most obvious choice of ingredients for a salad, but when you think about it, salty olives and sweet watermelon are the perfect pairing, playing off each other beautifully. I first had a salad like this in Morocco – it was served alongside the main course – tagine with lentils– and its fresh, subtle sweetness was the perfect accompaniment. If you don't mind dairy, little chunks of feta also work well with this dish. The labneh on page 125 is a great dairy-free option, but you'll need to prepare it a day ahead.

watermelon, black olive & rose water salad

600 g /1¼ lbs. watermelon, seeds and skin removed
2 teaspoons rose water
½ a red onion, thinly sliced
small handful fresh flat-leaf parsley and mint leaves, chopped, plus extra to garnish
100 g/⅔ cup black olives, stoned/pitted

Serves 4

Cut the watermelon into bite-size chunks and toss gently with 2 teaspoons of the rose water. Add in the red onion, flat-leaf parsley, mint and black olives and mix together.

Keep refrigerated until ready to serve. Sprinkle over the remaining herbs. If using feta or labneh, crumble or spoon a little over the top.

I love beet(root) roasted in the oven until tender with their skins still on, as they add a little crispy chewiness. The orange cuts through the earthy flavour of the beet(root) and keeps the quinoa nice and moist.

quinoa with mint, orange & beetroot

4 beet(root) (about
　400 g/14 oz.),
　scrubbed clean
extra virgin olive oil
sea salt and freshly
　ground black pepper
1 tablespoons good
　quality balsamic
　vinegar
300 g/1½ cups quinoa
1 teaspoon fennel seeds
1 teaspoon cumin seeds
2 oranges, one zested
1 unwaxed lemon,
　zested
large handful fresh mint
　leaves, chopped, plus
　extra for serving
small handful fresh flat-
　leaf parsley leaves,
　chopped

Serves 4–6

Preheat the oven to 200°C (400°F) Gas 6.

Trim the beet(root) stalks, but leave about 2.5 cm/1 inch on the top. Cut the beet(root) into 2 cm/¾ inch thick wedges, toss in 2 teaspoons of olive oil and season with salt and pepper. Place on a roasting tray and roast for 30–40 minutes until blistered and a sharp knife slides into the flesh with ease. Remove and toss with the balsamic vinegar while still hot.

Bring the quinoa to a boil in just under double its quantity of salted water. The moment it comes to the boil, reduce the heat to low and place the lid on top. Cook for about 12 minutes until all the water has been absorbed. Turn off the heat, remove the lid and let any remaining water evaporate. Remove to a wide plate or tray and leave to cool.

Place the fennel and cumin seeds in a dry frying pan/skillet over a medium heat for a few minutes until aromatic. Turn the heat off.

Grate the zest of one orange and set aside. Then, cut the top and bottom off both oranges, just down to the flesh, then place the oranges on their ends, cut-side down, and carefully, following the shape of the orange, cut the skin off in strips from top to bottom, removing all the pith. Then segment the oranges by cutting the flesh away from the membrane. Reserve the juice that has come out during preparation.

In a large bowl, combine the quinoa with the chopped herbs, spices, orange zest and lemon zest and season to taste with salt and pepper. Add in most of the beet(root) and orange segments (and reserved juice) and a little extra virgin olive oil. Combine and serve at room temperature with the remaining beet(root) and orange segments on top and a few fresh mint leaves sprinkled over.

Camargue red rice from southern France is a short-grain, slightly chewy rice, not dissimilar to the sticky short grain rice of South-east Asia, or brown rice from Korea and Japan. It is available in supermarkets and specialist shops and can be boiled until al dente, or cooked as you would do a risotto, feeding it with liquid. In a salad like this it is wonderful, not just a carby mass to accompany the other ingredients, but as a stand-out flavour and texture all of its own. If you are looking for a substitute, go for a short-grain Asian brown rice or farro. A client asked me to serve this dish with grilled halloumi through it, and that also worked well, if you don't mind the dairy.

camargue red rice salad
with black grapes, pecans & marjoram

80 g/½ cup pecan nuts
400 g/2 cups camargue red rice
2½ tablespoons good-quality balsamic vinegar
1 small garlic clove, crushed
2 teaspoons pure maple syrup
1 unwaxed lemon, zested

extra virgin olive oil
sea salt and freshly ground black pepper
½ a red onion, halved and very thinly sliced
150 g/5 oz. black grapes
small handful of rocket/arugula
handful of marjoram leaves, or oregano or basil

Serves 4-6

Preheat the oven to 180°C (360°F) Gas 4.

Place the pecan nuts on a roasting tray and roast the nuts for 3–4 minutes, until they're a shade darker and aromatic. Remove from the oven and set aside.

Bring a large saucepan of salted water to the boil, add in the rice and simmer for 20–25 minutes until cooked. It should still be a bit chewy. Strain off the water completely and leave the rice to dry out in the warm saucepan.

In a bowl combine together the vinegar, garlic, maple syrup, lemon zest and 3 tablespoons extra virgin olive oil. Season to taste with salt and pepper and then, when the rice has dried out but is still warm, pour over and combine. Add in the red onion, set-aside pecans and grapes and gently mix together. When ready to serve, combine together and mix in the marjoram. Taste and adjust the seasoning if necessary, then sprinkle a few rocket/arugula leaves over the top, before tumbling onto a large serving dish and serve at room temperature.

This stellar dish is the perfect way to finish off a few extra courgettes/zucchini that you might have left over.

courgette & onion bhajis
with sumac yogurt & pomegranate molasses

250 g/1 cup soy or Greek yogurt

1 tablespoon pure maple syrup

1 teaspoon sumac

sea salt

450 g/1 lb. courgette/zucchini, coarsely grated

70 g/$\frac{1}{2}$ cup chickpea/gram flour

40 g/$\frac{1}{3}$ cup rice flour

2.5-cm/1-inch piece of fresh ginger, peeled and finely grated

2 garlic cloves, peeled and crushed

1 teaspoon ground coriander

$\frac{1}{2}$ teaspoon cumin seeds

$\frac{1}{2}$ teaspoon fennel seeds

$\frac{1}{2}$ teaspoon mustard seeds

small handful fresh coriander/cilantro, chopped, plus extra to serve

175 g/6 oz. red onion, peeled, halved and thinly sliced

vegetable oil

1 tablespoon pomegranate molasses

Serves 4

In a bowl combine together the yogurt, pure maple syrup, sumac and a pinch of salt and set aside.

Place the grated courgette/zucchini in a sieve/strainer and press firmly to remove as much liquid as possible, then wrap in a clean dish towel and press firmly again to dry them off.

Place the flours into a large bowl and whisk in 80–100 ml/5–6 tablespoons of water to create a thick batter the consistency of double/heavy cream. Add in the ginger, garlic, spices, onion, set-aside courgette/zucchini, 1 teaspoon sea salt, most of the fresh coriander/cilantro and combine very well.

Pour 2.5 cm/1 inch of vegetable oil into a frying pan/skillet and set over a medium–high heat. If you have a cooking thermometer, it should be 180°C (350°F), if not test that the heat is right by dropping in a tiny amount of batter – if it turns golden and crisp after about 40 seconds it's ready. Carefully place separate heaped tablespoons of the mixture into the hot oil, shaping into circular mounds. Do not overcrowd the pan/skillet as it will bring the temperature of the oil down. Fry, turning once or twice until crisp and golden. Remove and drain on paper towels. Keep the bhajis warm while you fry the rest of them.

Serve immediately with the extra coriander/cilantro sprinkled on top. Dollop the sumac yogurt and pomegrantate molasses generously over each crispy bite.

These crab cakes are ideal as an appetizer, or you could make a platter of them with bowls of the mayonnaise to dip into. The saffron gives them an earthy and moorish flavour, which is lovely paired with the tangy lemon.

crab cakes
with saffron mayonnaise

300 g/10 oz., white crab
   meat
2 spring onions/scallions,
   finely chopped
small handful of fresh
   flat-leaf parsley, finely
   chopped
1 fresh red chilli/chile,
   deseeded and finely
   chopped
zest of 1 unwaxed lemon
   and 1–2 teaspoons
   freshly squeezed juice
100 g/1⅓ cups fresh
   white breadcrumbs,
   can be from spelt
   bread or gluten-free
   bread if coeliac/celiac
200 g/¾ cup
   mayonnaise (page
   106), or good-quality
   store-bought
sea salt and freshly
   ground black pepper
1 teaspoon saffron
   fronds/threads
1 egg, beaten
sunflower oil, for frying
handful of rocket/
   arugula leaves
extra virgin olive oil

Makes 12

Squeeze any excess liquid out of the crab meat and add to a bowl together with the spring onions/scallions, most of the parsley, chilli/chile, lemon zest, lemon juice, 50 g/⅔ cup of the breadcrumbs and 5 tablespoons of the mayonnaise. Season with sea salt and black pepper and mix everything together until well combined. Divide the mixture into 12 equal portions and form into slightly flattened balls. Refrigerate for 30 minutes.

Meanwhile, make the saffron mayonnaise. Place the saffron fronds/threads in a bowl and cover with 1 teaspoon of hot water. Give it a stir and leave to infuse for at least 5 minutes. Add to the remaining mayonnaise and stir to combine.

Dip the chilled crab cakes in the beaten egg and then roll in the remaining breadcrumbs until evenly covered. Set aside.

Pour 2.5 cm/1 inch of sunflower oil into a medium frying pan/skillet. Place over a medium heat until a piece of bread dropped into the oil browns in about 40 seconds. Carefully place the crab cakes in the oil and fry for 3 minutes on each side until crisp and golden. Remove with a slotted spoon and drain on paper towels.

Plate up the crab cakes with the rocket/arugula leaves twisted in and around them and the saffron mayonnaise on top. Drizzle over some extra virgin olive oil and scatter over the remaining chopped parsley. Serve immediately with lemon wedges on the side, if desired.

Sardines are full of flavour, but must be very fresh, so be sure to cook them within 24 hours of purchase. They are also a highly concentrated source of omega-3 fatty acids, making them a really healthy choice, too. Jerusalem artichokes, confusingly, have nothing to do with Jerusalem or artichokes. They are tubers, related to the sunflower family, and their name is derived from the Italian word for sunflower, girasole. Their sweet, nutty taste is perfect with sardines.

sardines with Jerusalem artichokes & salsa verde

600 g/1¼ lbs. Jerusalem
   artichokes, scrubbed
   and halved
extra virgin olive oil
sea salt and freshly
   ground black pepper
2 unwaxed lemons, halved
12 fresh sardines, cleaned,
   gutted and scaled

For the salsa verde:
2 tablespoons salted
   capers, soaked and
   rinsed
1 bunch each fresh flat-
   leaf parsley, mint and
   basil, leaves only
2 anchovy fillets
2 garlic cloves, peeled
zest of ½ unwaxed lemon
2 tablespoons red wine
   vinegar
150 ml/⅔ cup extra virgin
   olive oil
1 tablespoon Dijon
   mustard

Serves 4–6

Preheat the oven to 180°C (360°F) Gas 4.

For the salsa verde, thoroughly rinse the salted capers, then add them to a food processor together with the parsley, mint, basil, anchovies, garlic and lemon zest. Pulse on and off until well chopped, then remove to a bowl, add in the vinegar and slowly stir in the olive oil and mustard until well combined. Taste and season to taste.

Toss the scrubbed Jerusalem artichokes with just enough olive oil to coat and season with a few pinches of salt and pepper. Place on a roasting tray in one layer and roast in the centre of the oven for 35–40 minutes until golden and tender in the middle.

After the artichokes have been roasting for around 30 minutes, place a large frying pan/skillet on a medium-high heat. Brush the cut side of the lemon halves with olive oil, place cut-side down and fry on a high heat until moderately charred. Rub the sardines with just enough olive oil to coat them, and season with a little sprinkling of salt and pepper. Place the sardines in the pan/skillet and cook for 2 minutes on one side, then flip over and cook for a further 2 minutes.

Pile some of the Jerusalem artichokes onto a plate, top with sardines and spoon over some salsa verde. Serve immediately with the lemon halves.

Langoustines, the ones that look like mini lobsters, have the most delicious sweet and delicate flesh, perfect for a summer BBQ or if the weather is against you, on a pan inside. Here I serve it very simply with the Italian salsa agresto, which is not a million miles away from a pesto sauce, made with walnuts, almonds, parsley and basil. It is also great with pasta and drizzled over grilled vegetables.

langoustines with salsa agresto

65 g/½ cup fresh
   walnuts, plus a few
   extra to serve,
   chopped into chunks
35 g/¼ cup almonds
1 small garlic clove
1 small handful fresh
   flat-leaf parsley,
   leaves only
15–20 fresh basil leaves
extra virgin olive oil
½ an unwaxed lemon,
   zested and 2
   teaspoons freshly
   squeezed juice
sea salt and freshly
   ground black pepper
12 langoustines

Serves 4

Preheat the oven to 180°C (360°F) Gas 4.

For the salsa agresto, place the walnuts and almonds on separate roasting trays in the oven for about 5 minutes, until a shade darker and aromatic. Leave to cool and rub the walnuts to remove any loose skin.

Place the walnuts into a food processor with the almonds, garlic and herbs and blitz until you almost have a smooth paste, scraping down the sides every now and then. While blitzing, slowly pour in 100 ml/a scant ½ cup of olive oil and the lemon juice and zest. Season with ¼ teaspoon salt and some pepper. Taste and adjust if necessary.

Lay the langoustines on their backs and cut in half lengthways down the centre. Lightly oil the langoustines and season with a little salt and pepper. Heat a frying pan/skillet over a medium-high heat and place them flesh-side down on the pan/skillet. Cook for 2 minutes then flip over and cook for about 30 seconds.

Tangle 6 langoustine halves onto each plate, drizzle over the salsa agresto and scatter some of the chopped walnuts on top. Serve immediately.

My wife and I have eaten various takes on this dish in Korea, and have started to make it at home now. It is very delicate looking, but don't be fooled, the flavours are strong and vibrant. Make sure you buy exceptionally fresh tuna, it should be red and waxy-looking with no smell, explain to your fishmonger what you are using it for and they will be able to point you in the right direction.

tuna carpaccio
with tamari dressing

1½ tablespoons pure maple syrup

1 tablespoon tamari soy sauce

½ a lime, zested and 1 tablespoon of freshly squeezed juice

1 garlic clove, peeled and crushed

1 tablespoon extra virgin olive oil

½ teaspoon sesame oil

200 g/7oz. fresh tuna, sustainably sourced

1 small fresh red chilli/chile, deseeded and very finely sliced

1 tablespoon cress

Serves 4

For the tamari dressing, combine together the maple syrup, tamari, lime zest and juice, garlic, olive oil and sesame oil. Mix well and set aside.

Slice the tuna as finely as possible. If you are finding this difficult, you can make slightly thicker slices thinner by placing them between 2 pieces of clingfilm/plastic wrap or greaseproof/wax paper and gently rolling them out with a rolling pin or bottle. Don't get too enthusiastic with the rolling pin though, or you will end up with tuna mush!

Layer onto plates and scatter over the chilli/chile and cress. When ready to eat, drizzle over the sauce and serve immediately.

Meat & Poultry

I have never been a huge fan of meat or poultry served on its own,
like a slab of steak, for example. For me, it really needs to have
a beautiful herb sauce or spice rub to bring it to life. So here are
some of my favourite recipes, from vibrant Beef Rendang Curry
and Spiced Chicken with Quinoa, Lemon Zest & Rose Petals to
a meltingly soft slow-cooked Pulled Lamb Shoulder.

This rich Indonesian curry is absolutely worth the effort and cooking time, and actually, once you have everything in the pot it just sits there until cooked, so you can get on with something else. Rendang is quite a dry curry, so don't expect it to be swimming in sauce. The spice level is also on the high side, so reduce the quantity of dried and fresh chilli/chile if you prefer a milder curry.

beef rendang curry

4 tablespoons desiccated coconut

3 tablespoons coconut chips (optional)

2 tablespoons vegetable oil

2 cinnamon sticks

3 cardamom pods

800 g/1¾ lbs. stewing steak, cut into small chunks

1 tablespoon tamarind paste or lime juice

2 lemongrass stalks, outer leaves and ends removed, chopped

5 kaffir lime leaves, bruised

2 tablespoons coconut palm sugar

sea salt

400-ml/14-fl. oz. can coconut milk

200 ml/¾ cup beef, chicken or vegetable stock

½ fresh red chilli/chile, thinly sliced

steamed rice, to serve

pak choi/bok choy or other green vegetable (optional)

For the curry paste:

3 red chillies/chiles, deseeded

4 teaspoons chilli/hot red pepper flakes

1 red onion, chopped

5 shallots, chopped

5 garlic cloves, peeled

2 lemongrass stalks, outer leaves and woody ends removed, chopped

5-cm/2-inch piece fresh ginger, peeled and grated

1 tablespoon ground coriander

1 tablespoon ground cumin

1 teaspoon ground turmeric

Serves 4

Place all the curry paste ingredients, apart from the ground coriander, cumin and turmeric, in a food processor, together with 3 tablespoons of water, and blitz for a few minutes until it forms a paste. Scrape down the sides a few times. Remove to a bowl and stir in the ground spices.

In a dry frying pan/skillet, fry the desiccated coconut over a low-medium heat for a few minutes until just golden, then remove it and set aside. Heat the coconut chips (if using) in the same way and set aside.

Put the vegetable oil in a large casserole pot over a low heat. Add in the curry paste, cinnamon sticks and cardamom and cook gently for 15 minutes, stirring now and again, until fragrant and beginning to caramelize. Turn up the heat, add in the stewing steak and fry for a few minutes, stirring now and again, until the meat is just sealed and beginning to brown.

Add in the tamarind paste or lime juice, lemongrass, kaffir lime leaves, coconut palm sugar and 2 teaspoons sea salt. Cook for a couple of minutes until bubbling, then add in the coconut milk and stock and bring to a boil. Reduce the heat to very low and leave to simmer uncovered for 2 hours, stirring from time to time. Add in the set-aside desiccated coconut and continue to cook for a further 30 minutes until the meat is tender and most of the liquid has evaporated off. If serving with pak choi/bok choy, boil or steam until just tender and season with a little salt. Serve the curry in bowls with the toasted coconut flakes and sliced red chilli/chile sprinkled over and the rice on the side.

This dish is somewhat of an ode to one of my original mentors, the Michelin-starred chef Skye Gyngell, who I worked with for a few years when I first started out. Her approach to food and cooking is instinctive and considered, and I was incredibly privileged to have been able to learn from her. Although this dish is not exactly the same as those we cooked together, it is influenced by her style of cooking. Simple, great-quality ingredients cooked with care and patience.

quail with borlotti beans,
baby tomatoes & marjoram salmoriglio

300 g/1½ cups dried borlotti beans, soaked overnight (or fresh borlotti beans from their pods)

extra virgin olive oil

2 tablespoons red wine vinegar

6 garlic cloves, peeled

few sprigs of fresh rosemary

sea salt

20 baby plum tomatoes

4 quail

1 teaspoon ground cumin

1 teaspoon ground coriander

½ teaspoon ground cinnamon

freshly ground black pepper

1 handful fresh marjoram or oregano

½ a lemon

Serves 4

If using dried beans, cover with three times their volume in water and soak overnight. The next day, refresh with clean water and place in a large ovenproof pot. If using fresh beans, start from this stage. Do not add salt to the beans as this will prevent them from softening. Bring almost to the boil and then reduce to a gentle simmer. Cook for about 60–70 minutes or until almost tender (less for freshly podded, shelled beans).

Preheat the oven to 190°C (375°F) Gas 5. Drain most of the water from the beans, leaving about 75 ml/⅓ cup at the bottom. Add in 180 ml/¾ cup of olive oil, 2 tablespoons red wine vinegar, the whole garlic cloves, rosemary, tomatoes and a teaspoon of sea salt. Cover tightly with aluminium foil and a lid, then place in the oven for 30 minutes until the beans and garlic are soft. Remove and leave to cool a little. Taste and season with a little sea salt and red wine vinegar if necessary, keep warm.

Increase the oven temperature to 200°C (400°F) Gas 6. Rinse the quail and pat dry. Combine together the cumin, coriander, cinnamon and 1 teaspoon of salt and ½ teaspoon ground black pepper. In a large bowl, rub the quail with a little olive oil, then sprinkle over the spice mix and move around until the quail are well coated. Place on a baking sheet and roast in the centre of the oven for 20–25 minutes until golden and cooked through. Remove and leave to rest for 10 minutes.

While they are resting, make the marjoram salmoriglio. Place the marjoram in a pestle and mortar with ¼ teaspoon sea salt. Pound until you have a smooth paste. Add in a squeeze of lemon and slowly pour in 4 tablespoons of olive oil stirring as you go with the pestle.

Spoon some of the beans, tomatoes and garlic onto a plate or bowl, place one quail on top and drizzle over a little salmoriglio.

Poussin or baby chicken is lovely served as individual portions, or you could roast a whole chicken to share. Chermoula is a North African sauce Although traditionally served with fish, it's wonderful with almost anything.

roasted poussin
with new potatoes & chermoula

2 teaspoons dried chilli/ hot red pepper flakes

2 teaspoons ground coriander

sea salt and black pepper

2 tablespoons pomegranate molasses

zest of 2 unwaxed lemons

1 teaspoon coconut palm sugar

extra virgin olive oil

4 free-range poussin or 1 whole chicken

800 g/1$\frac{3}{4}$ lbs. new potatoes, halved

200 ml/1 scant cup chicken stock

For the chermoula:

2 teaspoons cumin seeds

3 garlic cloves, peeled

2 teaspoons smoked/ Spanish paprika

1 fresh red chilli/chile, deseeded and roughly chopped

1 handful fresh coriander/cilantro

1 handful fresh flat-leaf parsley leaves

$\frac{1}{2}$ teaspoon sea salt

1 tablespoon lemon juice

1 tablespoons pure maple syrup

60 ml/$\frac{1}{4}$ cup extra virgin olive oil

Serves 4

Preheat a fan oven to 180°C (350°F) Gas 4.

In a bowl combine the dried chilli/hot red pepper flakes with the ground coriander, a generous pinch of sea salt and freshly ground black pepper. Stir in the molasses, lemon zest, sugar and 1 tablespoon of the olive oil. Sit the poussin or whole chicken onto a large baking sheet and spoon over the molasses mixture, working it into all the crevices. Cut one of the lemons into 4 wedges and stuff into the cavity of the birds. Tie the legs together with twine.

Toss the halved new potatoes with 2 tablespoons of olive oil, season with salt and pepper, then place on another baking sheet. Place both trays in the oven and roast for 20 minutes. Carefully pour the stock into the baking sheet containing the poussin or whole chicken and continue to roast for 20–25 minutes, basting every 10 minutes, until the skin is crisp and juices run clear. If using a whole chicken, roast for a full 60 minutes. The potatoes should be crisp and golden by this stage.

For the chermoula, dry fry the cumin seeds for a few minutes until fragrant. Put the cumin seeds, garlic, smoked/Spanish paprika, chilli/chile, coriander/ cilantro, parsley and half a teaspoon of sea salt into a food processor and blitz. Slowly pour in the lemon juice, maple syrup and olive oil until combined. Set to one side.

Serve up the poussin or whole chicken and potatoes on a platter or in individual servings with the chermoula on the side or dolloped over, making sure to get plenty of it with each bite.

I love using quinoa as a base for salads or like here, spiced up and served with meat or fish. It's a fantastic source of protein, containing all the essential amino acids, and can be used as you would couscous. Millet is another option and is slowly gaining popularity; it has a slightly nutty flavour and works very well in dishes like this. The rose petals are a lovely addition and do certainly add flavour, but it is subtle, so feel free to omit if you like. For a vegetarian version, swap the chicken for roasted squash, and use vegetable stock instead.

spiced chicken
with quinoa, lemon zest & rose petals

4 chicken thighs and
   4 wings
extra virgin olive oil
sea salt
1 tablespoon ras el
   hanout (spice mix)
1 teaspoon dried chilli/
   hot red pepper flakes
1 red onion, halved and
   thinly sliced
1 teaspoon ground
   cinnamon
1 teaspoon ground cumin
3 garlic cloves, crushed
250 g/1¼ cups quinoa
12 dried apricots, sliced
zest of ½ an unwaxed
   lemon
1 handful each of fresh
   flat-leaf parsley, mint
   and coriander/cilantro
   leaves, chopped, plus
   extra to serve
1 tablespoon
   pomegranate molasses,
   or lemon juice
freshly ground black
   pepper
rose petals (optional)

Serves 4–6

Preheat the oven to 190°C (375°F) Gas 5.

Place the chicken in a large roasting tray and drizzle over 1 tablespoon of olive oil, just enough to coat them. Season with plenty of sea salt and sprinkle over the ras el hanout and chilli/hot red pepper flakes. Use your hands to massage the spices into the chicken. Roast for 25–30 minutes or until cooked through and the skin is crisp and golden. Keep warm.

In a large saucepan, gently sauté the red onion in a little olive oil until soft. Add in the cinnamon, cumin, garlic and 1 teaspoon salt and fry for another couple of minutes until aromatic. Add in the quinoa and just under double its quantity of water,

about 500 ml/2 cups. Bring to a boil, then reduce the heat to low and place the lid on top. Cook for about 12 minutes, then remove the lid and continue to cook until all the water has been absorbed and the quinoa is quite dry. Turn off the heat and add in the sliced apricots and lemon zest. Stir in the herbs, pomegranate molasses (or lemon juice), and season to taste with salt and pepper. Gently combine together.

Plate up the quinoa with the chicken on top and remaining herbs and rose petals scattered over.

Mapo tofu, the Chinese minced meat and tofu dish, is also very popular in Korea, albeit with a few Korean tweaks to the ingredients. The chilli and soybean pastes used in this recipe are easy to find in an Asian market and are popping up in some supermarkets. Or, you can substitute with normal mild chilli paste and Japanese miso paste.

Korean-style mapo tofu

sea salt
400 g/14 oz. tofu
sunflower oil
1 echalion/banana
  shallot, peeled and
  very finely chopped
1 teaspoon grated fresh
  ginger
1 garlic clove, crushed
350 g/12 oz. minced/
  ground beef
1 tablespoon Korean
  gochujang chilli paste
  (or other mild chilli
  paste)
1 tablespoon Korean
  doenjang soybean
  paste (or miso paste)
ground black pepper
175 ml/¾ cup beef or
  chicken stock
2 tablespoons mirin
2 tablespoons soy sauce
1 tablespoon coconut
  palm sugar or pure
  maple syrup
1½ teaspoons
  cornflour/cornstarch,
  whisked well into
  2 tablespoons water
1 tablespoon sesame
  seed oil
5 chives, thinly sliced
handful of coriander/
  cilantro leaves
rice to serve

Serves 4–6

Bring a pot of salted water to simmering point. Drain the tofu and cut into 2.5 cm/1 inch cubes. Carefully add the tofu to the water and simmer for 8 minutes. Then remove the tofu and leave to drain on a clean dish towel, being careful not to break the cubes.

Meanwhile, add 1 tablespoon sunflower oil to a large frying pan/skillet and place over a medium heat. When hot, add in the shallot and stir-fry for 1 minute, then add in the garlic and ginger and stir-fry for another minute, being careful not to let them burn. Add in the minced/ground beef, turn up the heat a little and stir-fry for 1–2 minutes. Add in the gochujang chilli paste, the doenjang soybean paste (or miso) and a few grindings of black pepper, combine together and stir-fry on a high heat for 1–2 minutes, breaking up the beef until almost cooked.

Add in the rest of the ingredients apart from the chives, coriander/cilantro and rice, and combine together. Gently add the drained tofu into the frying pan/skillet and carefully combine together ensuring you do not break up the tofu. Cook for 2–3 minutes until the sauce is thick and glossy.

Serve in bowls with the chives and coriander/cilantro leaves scattered over and the rice on the side.

NOTE: If you are avoiding refined cane sugar completely, bear in mind that most chilli/chile pastes will contain it, although the quantities of it will be very small per serving.

Slow and steady wins the race, and this lamb dish does just that, languishing in a low oven for hours, enshrouded in herbs and spices, until finally, it admits defeat and collapses at the merest touch.

pulled lamb shoulder
with orange and cinnamon pilaf

2 teaspoons coriander
  seeds
3 teaspoons cumin seeds
1 handful fresh mint
  leaves
2 oranges
4 garlic cloves, crushed
2 teaspoons ground
  cinnamon and 1 stick
  of cinnamon
sea salt and freshly
  ground black pepper
1.5 kg/3¼ lbs. lamb
  shoulder, most of the
  surface fat cut off
300 ml/1¼ cups chicken
  stock
200 ml/1 scant cup
  white wine (if you
  prefer to avoid alcohol
  you can use another
  200 ml/1 scant cup
  chicken stock)
300 g/1½ cups basmati
  rice
extra virgin olive oil
1 large onion, chopped
100 g/⅔ cup pine nuts,
  lightly roasted until
  golden
80 g/½ cup raisins
250 g/1 cup soy or
  Greek yogurt
1–2 fronds/threads fresh
  dill, chopped
1 pomegranate, seeds
  removed

Serves 4–6

First, make the marinade. Place the coriander seeds and ⅔ of the cumin seeds in a dry frying pan/skillet over a medium heat for about 3 minutes. Next, pound them in a pestle and mortar. Finely chop ⅔ of the mint, and add this to a bowl with the zest and juice of one of the oranges. Add the garlic, ground cumin, ground coriander, ground cinnamon and 1 teaspoon of salt and pepper and combine together. Make incisions all over the lamb and place in a large roasting tray; cover with the marinade and massage into the flesh. Cover and set aside for 1 hour, or in the fridge overnight.

Preheat the oven to 160°C (320°F) Gas 3. If the lamb was in the fridge overnight, remove 1 hour before cooking. Drizzle a little olive oil over the lamb, pour the stock and white wine into the tray, and cover very tightly with 2 layers of aluminium foil. Place in the centre of the oven for 5 hours. Remove and leave to stand for at least 15 minutes covered in the foil.

Rinse the rice well until the water runs clear. Add into a pot of boiling salted water, and return to the boil for exactly 6 minutes. Drain very well.

Place 2 tablespoons of oil in a frying pan/skillet (with a tightly fitting lid), over a medium heat, add in the onion, remaining 1 teaspoon of cumin seeds and stick of cinnamon. Cook for 10 minutes until the onions have softened. Peel 4 strips of zest from the remaining orange and add to the pan/skillet together with most of the pine nuts, turn up the heat and cook on high for 1 minute stirring constantly. Remove the onion and spice mix to a plate. Place the same pan/skillet on a medium heat and add 3 tablespoons olive oil and 2 tablespoons water. When hot, spoon in a thin layer of rice across the base of the pan/skillet. Add the raisins, onion and spice mix into the remaining rice and combine, then gradually spoon that on top of the base of rice, being careful not to squash it down. Using the handle of a wooden spoon, poke some holes in the rice so the steam can escape. Wrap the lid in a clean dish towel and cover. Leave the pan/skillet on a medium heat for 2 minutes, then reduce to the gentlest heat possible and cook for 30 minutes, without removing the lid.

Fill the kitchen sink ¼ full with cold water. When the rice is done, sit the pot straight into the water and leave for a few minutes. Invert the rice into a serving platter. Combine the yogurt and dill with a pinch of salt. Serve up the lamb, pulled into chunks with the rice alongside. Dollop over the dill yogurt and scatter the pomegranate seeds and remaining mint and pine nuts over the top.

You can buy really nice corn tortillas these days that are made with nothing more then masa harina (finely ground cornmeal), water and salt. They are delicious served soft, as I have done here, or if you want them crispy you can fry them in a little oil. This is the ultimate sharing dish, everything on the table with all the toppings ready to go. Feel free to add in any extra toppings that you particularly like.

beef tacos with avocado
& smoked paprika aïoli

mayonnaise (see page 106), but use 3 garlic cloves

½ teaspoon smoked/Spanish paprika

225 g/8 oz. sirloin/New York strip steak, removed from fridge 20 minutes before cooking

sea salt and freshly ground black pepper

olive oil

½ a red onion, thinly sliced

1 large or 2–3 small corn tortillas per person

1 head of baby gem/romaine lettuce

1 avocado, stoned/pitted, peeled and sliced

small handful of coriander/cilantro leaves

1 lime, cut into wedges

Serves 2

Once you have made the mayonnaise on page 106 (but with 3 crushed garlic cloves mixed in at the beginning), mix in the smoked/Spanish paprika and cover and refrigerate until needed.

Set a grill pan over a high heat. Drizzle a little oil over both sides of the steak and season with salt and pepper. When the pan is smoking hot, add the steak. For a steak about 2 cm/1 inch thick, fry for 2 minutes on each side for medium-rare, or longer if you prefer your steak well done. Remove the steak from the pan and leave to rest for 5 minutes.

Meanwhile, clean out the pan with paper towels, but be careful as it will still be hot. Add in the sliced onion and cook for a few minutes to soften. Once the steak has rested, slice into thin strips at an angle.

In a clean dry frying pan/skillet heat the corn tortillas for about 30 seconds on each side to warm through. To serve, place a couple of leaves of the lettuce on the tortillas, and top with the strips of steak, avocado, red onion, coriander/cilantro leaves and the aïoli dolloped over. Serve with the lime wedges to squeeze over.

Fish & Seafood

It took me a while to come around to fish. It wasn't until my teens
that I truly began to see the scope of what can be done with it,
and how hugely varied the tastes and textures can be, from light
and delicate Red Mullet with Coconut Rice to meaty and robust
Halibut with Coconut Creamed Corn. Here are some of the dishes
I cook most often.

This is a great dish for serving on the centre of the table and tucking into with friends. It works really well with salmon too. Farro is an ancient grain with a delicious slightly nutty flavour and a chewy consistency. It is high in protein and lower in gluten then wheat, so some people with an intolerance to wheat find they tolerate farro. Do not confuse it with spelt, which has a much harder shell and takes far longer to cook. Camargue red rice or short grain rice could also be used in its place.

trout stuffed with farro, dates & pine nuts

150 g/1 heaping cup farro
1 teaspoon red wine vinegar
extra virgin olive oil
sea salt and freshly ground black pepper
1 onion, finely chopped
1 garlic clove, crushed
1 handful coriander/ cilantro, chopped
1 handful flat-leaf parsley, chopped
30 g/¼ cup pine nuts, lightly roasted until golden
4 Medjool dates, stoned pitted and chopped
2 lemons, 1 zested and halved, the other cut into wedges
2 trout, cleaned, gutted and scaled

Serves 4–6

Rinse the farro thoroughly until the water runs clear. Add to a pot of cold water with a pinch of salt. Bring to the boil, then reduce heat and simmer for about 20–25 minutes until al dente. Farro has a lovely natural chewiness to it and you want to keep that texture, so taste it a few times until the consistency is just right. Drain off the water and immediately, while still hot, stir in the red wine vinegar and 2 tablespoons of the olive oil, season to taste with sea salt and black pepper.

Sweat out the onion in a frying pan/skillet with a tablespoon of oil over a medium heat until softened. Add in the garlic and cook for a further 1–2 minutes until aromatic. Add in the cooked farro and combine together with the coriander/cilantro,

most of the parsley, the pine nuts, Medjool dates and lemon zest. Taste and adjust the seasoning if necessary.

Preheat the oven to 200°C (400°F) Gas 6. Season the trout with salt and pepper, both inside and out. Place on a baking sheet with enough aluminium foil or parchment paper to create a parcel. Stuff the cavity of the fish with the farro, squeeze a little juice from the zested lemon halves around the fish and then nestle the lemon beside them. Seal the parcel tightly and bake in the centre of the oven for 15 minutes. Open the parcel exposing the fish and cook for another 5 minutes until the skin is slightly blistered and golden.

Serve on a platter with the lemon wedges and the remaining parsley.

Cauliflower, I am delighted to see, is beginning to swagger into the limelight. Recently a number of food writers have devoted their entire columns or recipes to this humble staple, and for good reason too, as there is far more that can be done with it than cauliflower and cheese. Here, it is served as a velvety smooth purée, so good it could even stand alone as a soup. Just add in some of the cooking liquid when blitzing until you reach the right consistency and top with the parsley oil.

sea bass, cauliflower purée & Swiss chard

extra virgin olive oil
1 onion, diced
4 garlic cloves, crushed
1 head of cauliflower,
    cut into florets, (about
    450 g/1 lb.)
vegetable stock, about
    800 ml/scant 4 cups
    or enough to cover
1 bunch Swiss chard,
    about 400 g/14 oz.,
    leaves removed from
    the thick stalks
4 sea bass fillets
small bunch of fresh
    flat-leaf parsley,
    finely chopped
sea salt and freshly
    ground black pepper

Serves 4

Pour 2 tablespoons of olive oil into a large frying pan/skillet over a medium heat. Add in the onion and sweat for 10 minutes until soft. Add in almost all of the garlic and cook for one minute, then add in the cauliflower, stir everything together and cook for 2 minutes.

Pour in enough vegetable stock to barely cover the cauliflower. Bring to a boil, reduce the heat and simmer until very soft. Drain off the stock through a sieve/strainer and discard. Put the cooked onion, garlic and cauliflower into a food processor. Blitz until you have a very smooth purée, adding in a drizzle of olive oil if needed. Taste and adjust the seasoning if necessary. If you are using fresh stock, you will need to season it properly with salt. If you're using stock cubes you may not need any added salt at all. Keep the mixture warm.

Place the chard stalks in a large pot of boiling salted water. Cook until just tender, but not limp. This should take about 3–4 minutes, depending on the thickness of the chard – taste a small piece to check. Remove, drain and season with a pinch of sea salt and a drizzle of olive oil. Boil the chard leaves in the same way, but remove after 2 minutes, drain well and season with salt and olive oil. Keep warm.

Place two non-stick frying pans/skillets over a medium-high heat. Drizzle a little olive oil over the sea bass fillets, just enough to coat both sides. Season with salt and pepper and when hot, place 2 fillets in each pan/skillet, skin-side down. Fry for 3 minutes without moving, then turn over and fry for a further 2 minutes.

Mix the chopped parsley and remaining crushed garlic with a pinch of sea salt and enough olive oil to create a loose parsley oil.

Spoon some of the cauliflower purée onto a plate, place a sea bass fillet on top with the chard twisted in and around the fish. Drizzle over some parsley oil and serve.

This subtle Cambodian curry remains largely unknown to western audiences. My friend Rhiannon who lives in Phnom Penh introduced me to amok while I was visiting Cambodia last year, and I've been hooked ever since. It is usually thickened with eggs and steamed in banana leaves, but I prefer it cooked on the stove without the eggs. I have given you a note below on how to cook it the more traditional way, if you like.

monkfish amok curry

vegetable oil
4 shallots, thinly sliced
400-ml/14-fl. oz. can
    coconut milk, plus
    extra to serve
2 tablespoons coconut
    palm sugar
5 teaspoons fish sauce
150 g/1 heaping cup
    green beans
400 g/14 oz. monkfish,
    cut into bite-size pieces
1 fresh red chilli/chile,
    thinly sliced
2 kaffir lime leaves, very
    thinly sliced
boiled or steamed
    jasmine rice to serve

For the amok paste:
2 fresh red chillies/chiles,
    deseeded
5 garlic cloves, peeled
2 stalks lemongrass,
    trimmed, outer leaves
    removed
5 shallots or 1 red onion
5 kaffir lime leaves
3-cm/1¼-inch piece
    galangal, peeled, or
    2-cm/¾-inch piece
    fresh ginger
1 teaspoon ground
    turmeric
zest of 1 lime

Serves 4

For the curry paste, add everything to a food processor with 3 tablespoons of water and blitz until you have a paste, scraping down the sides when needed. This will take at least a few minutes of constant blitzing.

Place a large pot with 2 tablespoons of vegetable oil over a medium heat. Add in the shallots and stir-fry for a few minutes until softened. Turn down the heat, add in the curry paste and cook gently for 5–10 minutes until fragrant. Add in the coconut milk, 200 ml/¾ cup water, sugar and fish sauce. Bring to a boil, reduce the heat to low and simmer for 3 minutes. Add in the green beans and fish and cook for a further 5–8 minutes until the fish is just cooked through and beans are tender. Ladle into a bowl and spoon a little coconut milk on top. Scatter over the sliced chillies/chiles and kaffir lime leaves and serve the rice on the side. If you like you can line the bowl with a banana leaf to serve. To do this, fold in the edges of the banana leaf and secure with a cocktail stick/toothpick.

TRADITIONAL METHOD: Preheat the oven to 180°C (360°F) Gas 4. Omit the green beans. After you have simmered the coconut milk, sugar and fish sauce for 5 minutes, remove and leave until almost cool. Add in 2 eggs and mix well to combine. Add in the fish pieces. Line a small ovenproof dish with a banana leaf and pour in the curry. Sit the dish on a baking sheet and place in the oven. Pour boiling water into the sheet surrounding the dish to create a bain-marie. Cook in the oven for 15 minutes. The curry should be a slightly set-custard consistency. Scatter over the sliced red chilli/chile and lime leaves and serve with rice.

Coconut rice is served more often as a dessert, but if you tone down the sweetness it works really well with savoury dishes too. I have served it with red mullet, its orangey pink hues beautiful against the white rice. You could also use sea bass or halibut here.

red mullet and coconut rice

175 g/1 scant cup jasmine rice, rinsed many times until water runs clear
350 ml/1 1/2 cups water
100 ml/scant 1/2 cup coconut milk (use leftovers for soups and porridge)
2 teaspoons coconut palm sugar
1/2 teaspoon salt
2 tablespoons vegetable oil
1 echalion/banana shallot, halved and thinly sliced

1 lemongrass, outer leaves removed and chopped very finely
1 fresh red chilli/chile, deseeded, 1/2 finely chopped and the other 1/2 finely sliced
2 garlic cloves, crushed
2 x 180 g/6 oz. red mullet or red snapper fillets, scaled and pin-boned
small handful of coriander/cilantro leaves
2 spring onions/scallions, halved and chopped

Serves 2

Put the rice, water, coconut milk, coconut palm sugar and salt into a saucepan with a lid and place over a medium heat. Bring to the boil, reduce the heat, cover and simmer gently for 15 minutes. Remove from the heat (keep the lid on) and leave to stand for 5 minutes.

Put 1 tablespoon of vegetable oil in a frying pan/skillet over a medium heat, add in the shallot, lemongrass and finely chopped red chilli/chile and fry gently for a minute or two to soften, add in the garlic and fry for a further minute. Add into the saucepan of rice and combine together. In the same pan, add in the remaining 1 tablespoon sunflower oil, season the fish with a little salt and pepper and when hot place in the pan skin-side down. Cook for 2 minutes until the skin is crisp, flip over and cook for another 1 minute.

Add most of the coriander/cilantro and spring onion/scallion into the rice and combine, plate up with the red mullet on top. Scatter over the remaining coriander/cilantro and spring onions/scallions and serve immediately.

This coconut-creamed corn is totally addictive, and works well as a side for most fish dishes, or on its own tossed with some salad for lunch. Try to buy sustainably-caught halibut, look out for the MSC (marine stewardship council) certification, or ask your fishmonger.

halibut & coconut creamed corn
with pak choi & chilli oil

4 corn on the cob/ears fresh corn

300 ml/1 $\frac{1}{4}$ cups coconut cream (thick cream from the top of coconut milk, you can also use coconut milk but it will be a little thinner in consistency)

sea salt

$\frac{1}{4}$ teaspoon paprika

handful of coriander/cilantro leaves

1 lime, zested and 1 teaspoon of juice

freshly ground black pepper

100 g/3 $\frac{1}{2}$ oz. pak choi/bok choy

extra virgin olive oil

1 fresh red chilli/chile, halved and deseeded

4 x 150 g/5 oz. halibut fillets, skin on

Serves 4

Using a serrated knife cut the corn kernels off the cob; the easiest way to do this is to stand the cob upright and cut down in a sawing motion.

Add the corn, coconut cream and 1 teaspoon of salt to a frying pan/skillet and set over a medium-high heat. Bring to the boil, then reduce the heat to low and simmer for about 20 minutes until the corn is tender and the coconut cream has reduced. Add in the paprika, coriander/cilantro, lime zest and juice and season with black pepper.

While the corn is cooking, bring a saucepan of water to the boil, add in a good pinch of salt and cook the pak choi/bok choy for a couple of minutes until just tender. I like them to still have a bit of bite. Drain and season with a drizzling of olive oil and a little salt. Keep warm.

Chop the chilli/chile very finely, then place in a small bowl with 3 tablespoons of olive oil and a pinch of sea salt and set aside.

Place 2 frying pans/skillets over a medium-high heat. Season the halibut fillets with sea salt and black pepper and drizzle olive oil over both sides of each fillet. Once the pans/skillets are hot, place 2 halibut fillets in each pan, skin-side down. Let them sizzle for about 2–3 minutes, then turn over and cook for another 2–3 minutes (depending on their respective thickness) until they are just cooked through.

To serve, spoon some of the creamed corn onto a plate, place the halibut on top and twist over the pak choi/bok choy. Drizzle over the chilli oil and serve immediately.

This is a very quick dish to make, but really full of flavour from the spice crust and fresh mango salsa. Feel free to use whatever spices you have to hand – fennel seeds and mustard seeds also work particularly well with the sea bass.

spice-crusted sea bass
with mango salsa

1 tablespoon coriander seeds

1 tablespoon cumin seeds

2 teaspoons caraway seeds

sea salt and freshly ground black pepper

1/2 teaspoon sweet/smoked paprika

1 egg white

4 x 180 g/6 oz. sea bass fillets

1 mango, not too ripe or soft

1/2 a red onion, about 35 g/1 oz., very finely chopped

1 fresh red chilli/chile, deseeded and very finely chopped

zest of 1 lime, freshly squeezed juice of 1/2 and 4 wedges to serve

1 small handful fresh mint leaves, chopped

Serves 4

In a pestle and mortar or spice/coffee grinder, roughly pound the coriander, cumin and caraway seeds with 1/2 teaspoon sea salt and 1/2 teaspoon black pepper. When it is roughly ground with little bits of whole seeds remaining, add in the smoked paprika and combine.

Whisk the egg white in a wide flat bowl. Coat the sea bass fillets one at a time with the egg white, then evenly sprinkle the spice mix over the fish on both sides.

Peel the mango, remove the stone/pit and dice the flesh. Place in a bowl and combine with the red onion, chilli/chile, lime zest and juice and mint. Season to taste with a little sea salt and pepper.

Pour 2 teaspoons of olive oil into a wide frying pan/skillet over a high heat, and when hot, fry the sea bass for 2–3 minutes on both sides. If you can't fit all of them on at once, fry in batches, as you don't want to overcrowd the pan/skillet.

Plate up the sea bass fillets with the mango salsa spooned over the centre. Serve immediately with a wedge of lime.

These homemade fish fingers may take a little longer to make, but they are absolutely worth the effort. I have made my mushy peas with garden peas; I realise this will come as a deep shock to the purists out there as I haven't used the traditional marrowfat peas, so by all means, if that is your preference, feel free to use them.

cod fish fingers
with mushy peas & mayonnaise

extra virgin olive oil
½ an onion, finely
    chopped
500 g/1 lb. shelled peas
1–2 garlic cloves, peeled
handful of fresh mint leaves
½ lemon, zested and cut
    into wedges, to serve
sea salt and freshly
    ground black pepper
100 g/¾ cup cornflour/
    cornstarch
2 eggs, beaten
250 g/2½ cups spelt or
    gluten-free
    breadcrumbs
500 g/1 lb. cod, skin
    removed and cut into
    sixteen 2.5 x 10 cm/
    1 x 4 inch fingers
vegetable oil, for frying

For the mayonnaise:
2 egg yolks
1 garlic clove, peeled
    and crushed
1 tablespoon freshly
    squeezed lemon juice
large pinch of sea salt
300 ml/1¼ cups good-
    quality extra virgin
    olive oil and 300 ml/
    1¼ cups sunflower oil,
    mixed together

Serves 4

To make the mayonnaise, you can use a food processor or whisk it by hand. Either way start off with all the ingredients in a bowl, apart from the oil. As you start to process/whisk, very slowly feed in the oil a little at a time until the mixture begins to emulsify and come together. Once this happens you can add the oil in a bit faster, but don't be tempted to pour it in too quickly or it will split. Have a little cup of boiling water ready in case this happens, as a few drops added in when it is looking like it might split usually brings it back together. When all the oil is blended in, taste, and if necessary, adjust the seasoning with a little more lemon juice and salt. Cover and refrigerate until needed.

To make the mushy peas, first place a frying pan/skillet over a medium heat with 1 tablespoon of olive oil, add in the chopped onion and sauté for 10 minutes until translucent, making sure not to let them colour. Keep to one side. Bring a large saucepan of water to the boil. Add in the peas and boil for 4 minutes

or until completely tender. Drain the peas and add most of them to a food processor with the onion, garlic, mint, lemon zest and 1 teaspoon of sea salt. Blitz the mixture, pouring in 1 tablespoon of olive oil at a time until you have a thick purée consistency. Remove to a bowl and stir in the remaining whole peas. Adjust seasoning with salt, pepper and a little more olive oil if necessary.

In a bowl combine the cornflour/cornstarch with 1 teaspoon salt and plenty of black pepper. Cover each cod finger in the flour, then in the beaten egg and finally roll in the breadcrumbs until evenly covered on all sides. Pour about 1 cm/½ inch of vegetable oil into a frying pan/skillet and place over a medium-high heat. When hot, fry the cod fingers in batches for about 2½ minutes on each side until crisp and golden. Remove, drain and keep warm.

Spoon some of the mushy peas onto a plate, arrange the cod fingers on top and serve with lemon wedges and the mayonnaise for dunking into.

Vegetarian Plates

If the average restaurant menu is anything to go by, one would be forgiven for thinking vegetarians only eat stuffed mushrooms and cheese risotto. It is such a shame, as there are so many delicious and memorable dishes that can be made with vegetables, grains and pulses, which are in no way bland or lacking. For the carnivores amongst you, I defy any of you not to fall in love with the Farinata, or glorious Pumpkin & Coconut Laksa.

We often cook laksa at home – a Malaysian noodle soup of sorts with sour, sweet, salty and spicy notes. You can buy laksa curry paste, but I have given you the recipe here as the flavour is much better and it keeps well in the fridge or freezer. Delica pumpkins, with their emerald green skin and vibrant orange flesh (it's practically an Irish flag, so you can't go wrong!), are great in this dish. However, they are not always available in supermarkets, so you can use any kind of squash instead.

pumpkin & coconut laksa

1 delica pumpkin or butternut squash, peeled, halved and deseeded

2 tablespoons olive oil
sea salt

2 tablespoons vegetable oil

4 shallots, thinly sliced

4 tablespoons of the curry paste (see below)

3 tablespoons coconut palm sugar or pure maple syrup

1½ teaspoons sea salt

zest and juice of 1 lime (about 2 tablespoons), plus another lime, cut into wedges, to serve

2 tablespoons tamarind paste (alternatively use another 2 tablespoons of lime juice)

2 x 400-ml/14-fl. oz. cans coconut milk

400 ml/1⅔ cups vegetable stock

handful of spinach leaves

200 g/6½ oz. rice noodles

½ a red onion, sliced

1 fresh red chilli/chile, deseeded and thinly sliced

small handful of fresh mint leaves

For the curry paste:

3 fresh red chillies/chiles, deseeded

2 teaspoons chilli/hot red pepper flakes

4 shallots, roughly chopped

5 garlic cloves, peeled

3 lemongrass stalks, outer leaves and woody ends removed, chopped

3-cm/1¼-inch piece fresh ginger, skin scraped off with a teaspoon

1 tablespoons ground coriander

1 teaspoons ground cumin

1 teaspoons ground turmeric

4 lime leaves (optional)

Serves 4

For the curry paste, add everything to a food processor with 6 tablespoons of water and blitz until you have a paste, scraping down the sides when needed. This will take at least 2 minutes of constant blitzing.

Preheat the oven to 180°C (360°F) Gas 4. Cut the pumpkin/squash halves into 3 cm/1¼ inch chunks, drizzle with the olive oil, season with salt and roast in the preheated oven for 30 minutes until cooked through.

Place a large pot with 2 tablespoons of vegetable oil over a medium heat. Add in the shallots and stir-fry for a few minutes until softened. Turn down the heat, add 4 tablespoons of the curry paste and cook gently for 5 minutes until fragrant. Add in the sugar or maple syrup, salt, lime zest and juice and tamarind paste. Cook for another few minutes until the sugar has dissolved and everything is sizzling. Add in the coconut milk and stock and bring to a boil. Reduce the heat, and simmer briskly for 10 minutes. Taste the soup and if necessary adjust the seasoning with a little more salt, lime juice or coconut palm sugar. You should be able to taste all the sour, salty, sweet elements quite strongly. Add in the cooked pumpkin/squash and the spinach leaves, stirring into the sauce until slightly wilted.

Cook the noodles in boiling water, according to the packet instructions. Ladle the soup into bowls and then add in a mound of noodles. Scatter over some of the red onion, chilli/chile and mint leaves and serve immediately with the lime wedges to squeeze over.

You would be forgiven for thinking that the only easy way to get your hands on teriyaki sauce would be to buy a bottle of the stuff in a shop. Actually, it is surprisingly easy to make yourself at home, with the added bonus of it not having any of the preservatives, sugar and flavourings that are so often added to mass-produced products. All you need is equal parts of soy sauce, mirin and sake or water, all of which are available in good supermarkets.

teriyaki tofu
with shiitake mushrooms & soba noodles

400 g/14 oz. block of firm tofu, drained

150 g/5 oz. fresh shiitake mushrooms, sliced

250 g/8 oz. soba noodles (see note, right)

vegetable oil

4 spring onions/scallions, finely sliced

1 teaspoons toasted black or white sesame seeds

For the teriyaki sauce:

6 tablespoons light soy sauce (or 5 tablespoons gluten-free tamari)

6 tablespoons mirin (look for the brands made without added sugar)

6 tablespoons sake or water

1½ teaspoons sesame seed oil

3 garlic cloves, chopped

4-cm/1½-inch piece ginger, peeled and chopped

Serves 4

Wrap the drained tofu block in a clean dish towel, sit on a plate with a wooden board (or other weighted object) on top and leave for 20 minutes to slowly press out any excess water.

To make the teriyaki sauce, combine together the soy sauce (or tamari), mirin, sake (or water), sesame seed oil, garlic and ginger in a bowl and set aside.

When the tofu has been drained, cut the block into 2.5 cm/1 inch cubes.

Place a large frying pan/skillet over a high heat, add in the teriyaki sauce and all the tofu. Cook on a high heat, turning the tofu now and again for 4 minutes until the sauce has reduced a little. Turn off the heat and set to one side.

Place a large pot of water on to boil. While that is heating up, add 3 tablespoons of sunflower oil to another frying pan/skillet and place over a high heat. Add in the

mushrooms and fry over a medium heat for 4 minutes until golden. Remove and stir into the teriyaki tofu.

Add the soba noodles to the water and cook as per the packet instructions, but test them 2 minutes before they are due to be ready – they should be just a little al dente. Drain thoroughly and add to the pan/skillet with the tofu and mushrooms and place over a high heat. Toss gently until hot and the noodles have absorbed the sauce. Add in most of the sliced spring onions/scallions, then serve in bowls with the remaining spring onions/scallions and sesame seeds scattered over.

NOTE: Despite being made almost entirely from buckwheat (wheat-free), soba noodles often contain wheat as well. However, you can find soba made entirely from buckwheat if you are avoiding wheat and gluten.

This Japanese dish is incredibly simple to make, yet the complex flavours of the miso paste would make anyone think you had been slaving over it for hours. Mirin is a fermented rice wine that is naturally sweet. Unfortunately most mirin available in supermarkets have glucose/corn syrup or sugar as one of the first ingredients, avoid these, proper mirin should have no added sugar at all. The Clearspring brand of mirin is a good example of what you should be looking for, or do a search online for other natural brands with no added sugar in your area. Nasu dengaku is lovely on its own with rice or as a side dish.

nasu dengaku
(miso-charred aubergine with honey yogurt)

250 g/1 cup coconut, soya or natural yogurt

1 tablespoon honey

2 large aubergines/eggplants

vegetable oil

3 tablespoons white miso

3 teaspoons coconut palm sugar

3 tablespoons mirin

2 teaspoons sesame seeds

1 spring onion/scallion, roughly sliced diagonally, to serve

Serves 4

Preheat a grill/broiler to medium.

Mix the honey into the yogurt and keep to one side. Cut the aubergines/eggplants in half lengthways and score the flesh. Drizzle over a little vegetable oil and rub into the flesh. Place on a grill/broiler pan under the grill/broiler and cook for 15 minutes on one side, then flip over and cook for another 15 minutes. Keep a close eye on them and if they look like they are beginning to burn, cover with aluminium foil. The white flesh should be soft, while the skin is still a little firm.

While the aubergines/eggplants are cooking, make the miso paste. Place the white miso, coconut palm sugar and mirin in a saucepan over a gentle heat and stir to combine for a couple of minutes. Once everything has come together and the mixture is warm, remove from the heat.

Once the aubergine/eggplant flesh is soft, carefully remove the pan. Turn the grill/broiler up to high and spread the miso paste evenly over the flesh side of the 4 aubergine/eggplant halves. Don't spread it too thick – you may not need to use all of the paste, depending on the size of the aubergines/eggplants. Return the aubergines/eggplants to the grill/broiler flesh-side up and cook for a few minutes until the miso paste begins to caramelize and bubble. Watch them carefully as they can burn very quickly.

Plate up and drizzle over some of the yogurt, serving the rest on the side. Scatter over the sesame seeds and spring onion/scallion slices and serve immediately.

When it comes to healthy and delicious vegetarian food, Indian cuisine really has it covered. This spinach kofta curry is just one such example, absolutely packed with flavour from all the spices and herbs, really comforting and warming, and yet good for you as well, with no cane sugar, refined wheat or dairy in sight. If you want the kofta to retain their crispiness, you can also serve them with the sauce on the side for dipping into.

spinach kofta curry

220 g/1¾ cups chickpea/gram flour
250 g/8 oz. spinach, stemmed and roughly chopped into small pieces
1 teaspoon ground coriander
¼ teaspoon red chilli powder
1.25-cm/½-inch piece fresh ginger, peeled and finely grated
1 fresh green chilli/chile, deseeded and finely chopped
1 onion (about 100 g/ 3½ oz.), finely chopped
1 garlic clove, peeled and crushed
pinch of baking powder
¾ teaspoon sea salt
vegetable oil, to fry
steamed rice, to serve

For the curry:
2 large tomatoes
2 fresh green chillies/chiles, deseeded
4 garlic cloves, peeled
2.5-cm/1-inch piece of fresh ginger, grated
1 medium onion, peeled and halved
3 tablespoons cashew nuts
3 tablespoons vegetable oil
¼ teaspoon cumin seeds
½ teaspoon ground turmeric
2 teaspoons ground coriander
½ teaspoon red chilli powder
½ teaspoon garam masala
1 teaspoon sea salt
handful of chopped coriander/cilantro leaves

Serves 4–6

For the koftas, sift the chickpea/gram flour into a large bowl, then stir in 120 ml/½ cup water until you have a very thick batter with no lumps. Add the spinach to the batter with the rest of the ingredients and stir very well to combine. It should be thick with the spinach bound together by the batter – if it is too dry, add a little water; if it's too wet, add a little flour.

Add 1 cm/⅜ inch of vegetable oil to a wide frying pan/skillet over a medium heat. When hot, place heaped tablespoons of the batter into the oil, using 2 spoons to shape into mounds. Cook in batches for 7–8 minutes, turning a few times until deep golden brown. Remove with a slotted spoon and drain.

For the curry, place the tomatoes, chillies/chiles, garlic, ginger, onion and cashew nuts in a food processor and blitz for a few minutes until smooth. Pour the oil into a wide frying pan/skillet over a medium heat. Once hot, add in the cumin seeds, ground turmeric and ground coriander and fry for about 30 seconds. Add in the nut paste from the food processor, chilli powder, garam masala and salt and stir well to combine. Turn the heat down to low and cook for about 5 minutes, stirring regularly until the oil begins to separate from the mixture.

Add in 400 ml/1⅔ cups water and bring to a boil, then simmer for 5 minutes. Increase the heat to low-medium, add in the koftas and simmer for about 4 minutes until they have absorbed some of the water and the curry has thickened. Add in most of the coriander/cilantro and stir through. Serve in bowls with the remaining coriander/cilantro and the rice on the side.

Pad Thai seems such an obvious recipe these days, the ubiquitous take-away staple, sticky, sickly sweet and nothing like the fresh, vibrant dish found all over Thailand. On the surface, it seems a relatively simple dish, in practice however, it is quite easy for it to turn into a congealed, under-seasoned, lump. The easiest way to avoid this is to keep a close eye on the noodles, separating them while cooking to avoid sticking together. I also make the sauce in advance, rather then add ingredients individually, which makes it easer to control the overall flavour.

Pad Thai

4 tablespoons light soy sauce

3 tablespoons coconut palm sugar

1½ tablespoons tamarind paste mixed with 1½ tablespoons water or 3 tablespoons freshly squeezed lime juice

200 g/6½ oz. flat rice noodles

vegetable oil

100 g/3½ oz. pak choi/bok choy, leaves separated and sliced lengthways

3 garlic cloves, crushed

100 g/1⅓ cups beansprouts

1 fresh red chilli/chile, deseeded, ½ chopped and ½ finely sliced

6 spring onions/scallions, finely sliced

2 eggs, beaten

lime wedges, to serve

handful coriander/ cilantro leaves, to serve

50 g/2 oz. cashews or peanuts, roasted, to serve

Serves 2

To make the sauce, place the soy sauce (or fish sauce if you're not vegetarian), coconut palm sugar and tamarind or lime juice in a small saucepan and place over a medium heat. Warm through until the sugar dissolves completely then remove from the heat.

Soak the noodles in hot water for about 5–7 minutes until tender, but not soft.

Put 2 tablespoons of vegetable oil in a large frying pan/skillet or wok over a high heat. Add in the pak choi/bok choy, garlic, beansprouts, the chopped chilli/chile and 4 of the spring onions/scallions. Stir-fry for about 1 minute until the garlic is aromatic, keeping an eye on it so it does not burn. Add the noodles to the pan with 1 tablespoon of water, tossing them around and separating any noodles that are sticking together. Add in the sauce and cook, tossing occasionally, until the noodles have soaked up most of the liquid and are cooked through. Taste to make sure.

Push the noodles slightly over to the side to make way for the beaten egg. Scramble it in the pan and stir through the noodles. Taste, and if necessary, add more seasoning. Plate up with the remaining spring onions/scallions, sliced chilli/chile, coriander/cilantro and cashew nuts sprinkled over the top. Serve immediately with the lime wedges on the side.

Pissaladière, like socca (see the Farinata recipe on page 122), is another favourite recipe of mine from the south of France. The base is made with bread or pizza dough, except not rolled out quite as thin. It is the ultimate example of how glorious a pizza-type dish can be without the use of cheese. The slow cooked onions are essential for a good pissaladiére, so don't be tempted to whack up the heat to try and speed things up; this is one of those things that you just can't cheat.

pissaladière

250 g/2 cups white spelt flour

1 teaspoon easy blend dried yeast (about ½ a 7 g sachet)

1 tablespoon coconut palm sugar

extra virgin olive oil

1 teaspoon sea salt, plus a little extra to serve

5 large onions (about 1 kg/2¼ lbs.), peeled and sliced thinly

few sprigs of thyme

2 garlic cloves, crushed

25 stoned/pitted black olives

Serves 4–6

Place the flour, yeast, coconut palm sugar and salt in a large mixing bowl. Add in 125 ml/½ cup of warm-hot water and 2 tablespoons of olive oil. Bring together and then with one hand, lift the entire dough into the air and slap it very firmly back down into the bowl. Repeat this movement 10 times. It will be sticky at this point, but tip it out onto a lightly floured work surface and knead for 6–8 minutes until it is no longer as sticky and has become smooth in appearance. Use a little more flour as you go to keep it from sticking, but make sure you use the minimum possible. Place in a lightly oiled bowl and leave to rise in a warm place (near a turned-on oven or radiator is best) for an hour, or until the dough has doubled in size.

Meanwhile, place the onions, thyme and 4 tablespoons olive oil in a large heavy-based frying pan/skillet and place over a low heat. Cook very gently for 30 minutes, add in the garlic and cook for another 10 minutes, stirring now and again until the onions are very soft and sweet, but not brown. Set aside.

Beat back the dough, tip out onto a lightly floured surface and roll into either 4 small or 1 large rectangular shape. Carefully move onto a lightly oiled baking sheet. Leave to rise for another 30 minutes.

Preheat the oven to 245°C (475°F) Gas 9. After the second rising, dimple the dough with your fingertips, leaving the edges as they are. Cover with the onions and the olives. If you are not vegetarian, pissaladiére is often topped with anchovies, traditionally in a criss-cross pattern. Personally, I don't really like my pissaladiére looking like a stain glass window so I leave it more rustic-looking.

Bake in the oven for about 20 minutes, until the dough is cooked and the edges are crisp and golden. Drizzle over a little olive oil, a sprinkling of sea salt and then serve immediately.

In 'The Guilt-Free Gourmet' I gave you a Socca recipe, one I had found in its native Nice many years ago; this particular one was thin and almost crêpe like. Well, if you hop on the train in Nice and rumble along the Cote D'Azur with the mesmeric Ligurian sea on your right-hand side, you will find yourself, a little over an hour later, in Ventimiglia, Italy. Here, you will find a thicker Italian version, known as farinata. Whichever one you try, whether it be in France or Italy, it is nearly always cooked on a very large cast-iron pan in a searingly hot wood-fired oven, then served very simply with some black pepper. Here I have given you two equally satisfying options, a more traditional method, and an instant one.

farinata
with red pepper & tender-stem broccoli

400 g/14 oz. tender-stem
  broccoli/broccolini
1 red onion, very finely
  chopped
small jar roasted red
  (bell) peppers
½ teaspoon dried red
  chilli/hot red pepper
  flakes, or urfa chilli
  flakes
sea salt and freshly
  ground black pepper

For the batter:
300 g/2⅓ cups
  chickpea/gram flour,
sea salt
2 sprigs rosemary, leaves
  only, roughly chopped
extra virgin olive oil, plus
  regular olive oil for
  frying
480 ml/2 cups sparkling/
  soda water (for instant
  version only – see right)

Serves 3–6

For the more traditional version of farinata, make the batter by placing the chickpea/gram flour, 1 teaspoon sea salt (ground to a powder) and the rosemary leaves in a large bowl. Slowly whisk in 4 tablespoons extra virgin olive oil and 415 ml/1¾ cups plain water, ensuring that there are no lumps. Cover and leave at room temperature for at least 4 hours (or ideally overnight).

Preheat the oven to 240°C (465°F) Gas 9. Bring a saucepan of salted water to a boil, cook the broccoli/broccolini for about 3 minutes, or until just tender. Drain, drizzle over a little olive oil and set aside. Put 2½ tablespoons of olive oil in a 24 cm/10 inch non-stick ovenproof frying pan/skillet and place on a high heat. Only when extremely hot, almost smoking, ladle on ⅓ of the batter, which should be about 1 cm/⅜ inch thick, swirling around so it is evenly distributed. Leave on the high heat for exactly 1 minute, then place in the oven and cook for 5 minutes, or until it is set and the underside is crispy. Flip onto a large plate so the crispy underside is uppermost and drizzle over a very generous amount of good extra virgin olive oil. Sprinkle over some red onion, and place some red pepper and broccoli on top. Finally sprinkle over chilli/hot red pepper flakes and a little sea salt and pepper and serve.

For the instant version of farinata, use sparkling water instead when making the batter, as this gives the pancake a lighter texture without having to leave it to ferment. Fry in a pan/skillet as above, but instead of putting the pancake in the oven after 1 minute, turn the heat down to medium and fry for a couple of minutes until the base is set and the top is drying out, then carefully flip over and cook for another few minutes. When the pancake is cooked through, slide off and serve as above with the various toppings.

I made this dish for a client's dinner party who was desperate for a vegetarian main dish that didn't involve mushrooms, pasta or cheese. I will admit that if you make everything from scratch it is time-consuming and fairly labour-intensive, but the end result is worth it. I do also offer alternatives if you feel like life is too short (see short cuts below).

onion squash
with cavolo nero, Puy lentils, labneh & za'atar

1 onion squash or butternut squash, halved, deseeded and cut into 4 cm/1½ inch wedges
extra virgin olive oil
250 g/8 oz. baby plum or cherry tomatoes
300 g/1½ cups Puy/French lentils
1 head of cavolo nero cabbage, stalks removed
4 teaspoons red wine vinegar
1 tablespoon soy sauce
sea salt and freshly ground black pepper

For the labneh:
500 g/16 oz. soy or Greek yogurt
½ teaspoon sea salt

For the za'atar:
4 tablespoons dried thyme
1 tablespoon fresh oregano, finely chopped
2 tablespoons toasted sesame seeds
1 tablespoon ground sumac
¼–½ teaspoon sea salt

muslin/cheesecloth

Serves 4

For the labneh, fold the muslin/cheesecloth in two and line a large, deep bowl. Stir the salt into the yogurt and pour into the muslin-/cheesecloth-lined bowl. Pull up the corners and secure together with an elastic band. Suspend this yogurt parcel from a wooden spoon placed across the top of the bowl, ensuring it is not touching the bottom as you do not want it sitting in the water that strains off. Cover and leave in a cool place for at least 24 hours. If you haven't got a cool kitchen storage area, put the bowl in the refrigerator. The longer you strain it, the thicker it will become.

To make the za'atar, pound half the thyme, sesame seeds, sumac and salt. Add in the remaining half of the 4 ingredients listed above and all of the chopped oregano. Mix together and store in an airtight container.

Preheat the oven to 180°C (360°F) Gas 4. Toss the squash wedges and tomatoes in a little olive oil and season. Roast the squash for 35–40 minutes. Fifteen minutes before the squash is done, add in the tomatoes and continue to cook. The tomatoes should have just burst open by the time the squash is cooked through.

Bring the lentils to a boil in a large pot of cold water. Reduce the heat and simmer for about 20 minutes or until just tender with a little bite. Add in the cavolo nero leaves in the last 3 minutes of cooking. Drain and stir in the red wine vinegar, soy sauce and 3 tablespoons of olive oil. Taste and adjust the seasoning if necessary.

Arrange the squash on a plate, with the lentils, cavolo nero and tomatoes in and around them. Dollop over the labneh, sprinkle over some za'atar and a little olive oil. Serve immediately.

SHORT CUTS
• Buy packs of pre-cooked lentils and season as per the recipe
• Instead of labneh, simply season either the soya or natural yogurt with salt and pepper, drizzle over and top with za'atar
• Buy ready-made za'atar from good supermarkets or delicatessens

Gnocchi is a lovely alternative to pasta and is easy to make – you just have to make sure you only add just enough flour to bring the potato together, otherwise it can become overly chewy.

gnocchi with tomato, parsley and almonds

500 g/1 lb. evenly
  sized floury
  potatoes, like
  Désirée, Maris
  Piper or russets
½ teaspoon finely
  grated nutmeg
sea salt and freshly
  ground black
  pepper
1 egg, beaten
125 g/1 cup white
  spelt flour

200 g/6½ oz. cherry
  tomatoes
extra virgin olive oil
40 g/¼ cup almonds
4 anchovy fillets
2 garlic cloves
2 teaspoons capers,
  rinsed thoroughly
  and drained
handful fresh flat-leaf
  parsley leaves

Serves 4

Preheat the oven to 200°C (400°F) Gas 6. Prick the potatoes and bake in the oven for about an hour or until fully cooked and tender. Remove from the oven (leave it on), and while still hot, using a knife, fork and spoon if necessary, cut open the potato and scoop the flesh into a bowl – you should have about 320 g/ 1⅔ cups. Mash very well and then press through a sieve/strainer. Season with the nutmeg, ½ teaspoon finely ground sea salt and black pepper, then stir in most of the egg. Add in the flour a few spoonfuls at a time, and knead until you have a smooth dough. Depending on how wet the dough is, you may need a little more or less of the egg and flour, so add it in bit by bit to get it just right, smooth, but not sticky. Divide the dough into 4, and roll each piece into long sausage shapes, a little less then 2.5 cm/1 inch wide. Use some flour to prevent it from sticking. Cut into little lengths, about 2.5 cm/1 inch for each one. Using a floured fork, press down onto each piece to leave little ridges and shape into rectangles.

Place a large saucepan of water on to boil. While that is heating up, make the sauce by tossing the tomatoes with a little oil and place on a baking sheet in the oven for 12–15 minutes until their skins burst open. In the last 6 minutes, add the almonds to the oven on a separate baking sheet. Remove both from the oven and add to a food processor with the anchovies, garlic, capers, most of the parsley and 4½ tablespoons olive oil. Blitz until the almonds have broken into small pieces. Taste and adjust the seasoning if necessary.

Cook the gnocchi in batches in the boiling water. Stir in and boil for a couple of minutes or until they rise to the top. Strain thoroughly and gently combine together with the tomato sauce. Plate up with the remaining parsley sprinkled over and a little drizzle of extra virgin olive oil.

Cakes & Desserts

Everyone wants to be able to indulge now and again, and what better way to do so then with some of these more natural and unrefined, yet no less delicious, sweet treats. From Chocolate and Pistachio Cake with Salted Caramel, to Winter Granita of Blood Orange & Persimmon, there is a decadent cake or dessert in here to suit every occasion.

*My wife, having seen a similar cake in a shop window, requested
a guilt-free version for her birthday party, and this was the end result.
The coconut cream frosting is easy to make and absolutely delicious.*

fruits of the forest cake
with rose water & coconut cream frosting

4 eggs
225 g/2 cups white spelt
 flour
225 g/1 cup sunflower
 butter
190 g/6½ oz. xylitol
2 teaspoons pure vanilla
 extract
2½ teaspoons baking
 powder
pinch of sea salt
400 g/14 oz. raspberries,
 redcurrants,
 blueberries and
 strawberries – halved
 and hulled

For the coconut cream
frosting:
2 x 400-ml/14-fl. oz. cans
 of coconut milk,
 refrigerated overnight
 to let the milk separate
 from the cream
1½ tablespoons xylitol
2 tablespoons coconut
 oil, melted
3 unwaxed lemons, very
 finely zested

*2 x 20 cm/8-inch cake
 pans, greased and lined
 with parchment paper*

Serves 10

For the coconut cream frosting, first remove the cans of coconut milk from the fridge. Open and carefully scoop out only the very thickest, almost solid, white cream, leaving the thinner and clear coconut cream and water behind. This can be used for porridge, soups, curries etc. You should have about 400 ml/1⅔ cups of the thick cream from the 2 cans. Put the 1½ tablespoons xylitol in a spice/coffee grinder and mix so that it forms a powder – it needs to be as fine as icing/confectioners' sugar to work. Combine together the coconut cream with the melted coconut oil, powdered xylitol (reserving ½ a teaspoon or so to sprinkle over the finished cake) and lemon zest. Refrigerate while you make the cake.

Preheat the oven to 180°C (360°F) Gas 4. Place the eggs, spelt flour (no need to sift), sunflower butter, 190 g/6½ oz. xylitol, vanilla extract, baking powder and salt into the bowl of a food processor (or mix by hand), until everything is smooth and has just combined together. Do not overmix or the cake will be tough.

Divide the mixture evenly between the 2 prepared cake pans and level out. Bake in the centre of the oven for 22–25 minutes, until golden, and firm with a slight spring to the touch. Leave to cool for 10 minutes then remove from pans. Once completely cool, (otherwise the coconut cream will melt), ice the top side of one of the cakes and cover with berries. Carefully ice the underside of the other cake and position on top of the other cake. Ice the top of this cake this time decorating with the remaining berries. Sift over the reserved powdered xylitol.

TIP: When buying coconut milk to use for cream, read the ingredients and buy one that has coconut extract of at least 50–60 %, but the higher the better. This frosting will not work unless the coconut cream is very thick and almost solid after refrigeration. Some brands of coconut milk are treated so they stay as liquid even when refrigerated, so test out a few brands to find the best one. Any brands that have not set can be used for curry, porridge, soups etc.

Surely the phrase 'death by chocolate' must have been dreamt up by someone eating a cake like this? It is so rich and decadent that there is every possibility you might just keel over upon tasting it, so completely overcome by the chocolatey goodness. What I love most about this cake however, is the fact that absolutely no flour, cane sugar or dairy is used, and yet it tastes far better then the majority of chocolate cakes I have ever had the pleasure of gorging on.

chocolate & pistachio cake
with salted caramel

250 g/8 oz. dark/bittersweet chocolate, minimum 70 % cocoa solids (see tip below)

225 g/1 cup sunflower butter

100 g/^{2}/$_3$ cup shelled unsalted pistachio nuts, plus 3 tablespoons, to serve

100 g/^{2}/$_3$ cup stoned/pitted Medjool dates

6 eggs

300 g/1^1/$_2$ cups coconut palm sugar

sea salt

1 teaspoon pure vanilla extract

200 ml/^{3}/$_4$ cup coconut milk

unsweetened cocoa powder, to dust

22-cm/9-inch loose-bottomed cake pan, greased and lined with parchment paper

Serves 12

Preheat the oven to 160°C (325°F), Gas 4.

Melt the chocolate and sunflower butter in a heatproof bowl over barely simmering water. While that is melting, place the pistachio nuts in a food processor and blitz until very finely ground. Remove to a bowl. Add the Medjool dates and 2 of the eggs to the processor and blitz until the dates are finely chopped. Remove to a separate bowl and whisk in the remaining 4 eggs. Set aside.

When the chocolate and butter have completely melted, whisk in 200g/1 cup of the coconut palm sugar and ¼ teaspoon of sea salt while still sitting over the simmering water. Once dissolved, remove from the heat and whisk in the vanilla extract and the set-aside egg and date mixture. Make sure to whisk very quickly and continuously until the eggs have fully incorporated, resulting in a thick, shiny mixture, otherwise the eggs will be lumpy. Add in the ground pistachio nuts and mix well to combine.

Pour into the prepared cake pan and bake in the centre of the oven for about 35 minutes or until the cake is set but with a little wobble in the centre. Leave to cool completely, then remove from the pan.

For the caramel, place a saucepan with the coconut milk and remaining 100 g/½ cup coconut palm sugar over a medium-high heat. Bring to a boil, stirring all the time, then reduce the heat, add in a large pinch of sea salt and simmer for 10 minutes, stirring on and off, until you have a thick and viscous caramel.

Roughly chop the remaining pistachio nuts. To serve, dust the cake with cocoa powder, then pour over the caramel and sprinkle with the pistachio nuts and a little sea salt. It is important that you serve this cake in thin slices, unless you are planning on killing your guests.

TIP: Dark/bittersweet chocolate still has a very small amount of sugar cane in its ingredients, so to avoid it completely you can also find dark chocolate sweetened with natural sweeteners in health food stores.

When I lived in New York, I used to indulge in a killer chocolate and peanut butter tart. Here is my natural (but no less indulgent) version.

chocolate & nut butter tart

25 g/3 tablespoons whole almonds, roasted
1 tablespoon coconut palm sugar
100 g/3½ oz. dark/bittersweet chocolate, sweetened with natural sugar

For the base:
80 g/½ cup pecans
110 g/4 oz. oat cakes/biscuits
90 g/3 oz. dried stoned/pitted dates
1 tablespoon coconut oil
4 teaspoons cocoa powder
1 tablespoon pure maple syrup
pinch of sea salt

For the nut butter layer:
175 g/1¼ cups stoned/pitted Medjool dates
5 tablespoons rice milk
200 g/¾ cup smooth nut butter
2 tablespoons coconut oil, melted
2 tablespoons pure maple syrup

For the chocolate layer:
200 g/6½ oz. avocado
3 tablespoons cocoa powder
4½ tablespoons pure maple syrup
pinch sea salt
2 tablespoons coconut oil, melted

Serves 10–12

Grease a 20-cm/8-inch loose-bottomed cake pan with vegetable oil. Lightly roast the pecans at 180°C (360°F) Gas 4 for 3–4 minutes or until they are a shade darker and aromatic. Leave to cool. Place all the base ingredients in a food processor and blitz until it sticks together when pressed between your fingers. Press firmly into the cake pan so you have an even and smooth base. Place in the fridge to set for 30 minutes or the freezer for 15 minutes.

For the nut butter layer, blitz the dates and rice milk to a smooth paste in a food processor. Add in the nut butter and blitz for a couple of seconds until just combined. Pour in the coconut oil and maple syrup and blitz for another few seconds until incorporated. Don't blitz for any longer as the coconut oil will split away from the oil in the nuts. Maple syrup also causes nut butter to seize and become thicker, so don't worry if it becomes firm. Add this to the base of the cake pan and level out with the back of a spoon dipped in boiling water. Cover and place in the freezer while making the chocolate layer.

To make the chocolate layer, add the avocado, cocoa powder, maple syrup and salt to a food processor.

Blitz until smooth then pour in the melted coconut oil and blitz briefly to combine. Take the cake pan out of the fridge or freezer and spoon on the chocolate mixture and level out. Return to the fridge or freezer.

Place the roasted almonds in a dry pan/skillet with 1 tablespoon coconut palm sugar, heat through until the sugar melts and coats the nuts. Leave to cool and roughly chop.

To make chocolate curls, melt the chocolate and spread out in a thin layer on a large flat baking sheet. Leave aside until just set, but not solid, and check regularly as it is important it does not set completely. Using a flat-edged spatula, scrape the chocolate from the baking sheet, pushing away from you. You can use a hairdryer to get it back to the right consistency if it is too firmly set. Place the curls in the fridge to set and then tumble onto the tart with the almonds. Keep the tart in the freezer and remove 30–45 minutes before serving.

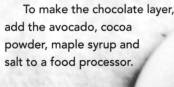

I was not exposed to the delights of baklava until my teens, while on a trip to London. I remember my first taste, in a little Turkish café, the crisp layers of filo/phyllo and syrup-laden nuts – it was almost too good, and it pained me to ration out my stash after I returned home to Dublin. Years later, I developed this recipe in a bid to create something just as delicious, but without all the refined cane sugar and butter. I have used coconut oil and maple syrup, which are just wonderful with the spices and nuts. Filo/phyllo pastry is very difficult to make by hand, so you have to rely on the shop-bought brands (not gluten-free).

baklava

200 g/1⅓ cups shelled unsalted pistachios, plus 1 tablespoon extra to serve
100 g/⅔ cup each of whole almonds and pecan nuts
150 g/¾ cup coconut palm sugar
good pinch of sea salt
½ teaspoon ground cinnamon
¼ teaspoon ground cardamom
5 tablespoons coconut butter or oil, melted
20 filo/phyllo sheets, cut into 15 x 25-cm/ 6 x 12-inch rectangles

For the syrup:
180 ml/¾ cup pure maple syrup
120 ml/½ cup water
1 cinnamon stick
freshly squeezed juice of ½ an orange
freshly squeezed juice and zest of ½ a lemon
2 cardamom pods, bashed open

Serves 12

For the syrup, place all the ingredients in a saucepan and bring to a boil. Reduce the heat to low and simmer for 5 minutes until slightly reduced. Remove from the heat and leave to cool. Strain through a sieve/strainer and refrigerate.

Preheat the oven to 180°C (360°F) Gas 4. Line a 15 x 25 cm/6 x 10 inch cake pan with parchment paper. Place half the nuts and the coconut palm sugar, salt, ground cinnamon and cardamom in a food processor. Blitz until very finely chopped. Add in the remaining nuts and blitz until finely chopped, but not quite as finely as the first half, so they have a bit of a bite.

Using a pastry brush, brush the parchment paper with a little of the melted coconut butter or oil. Place one filo/phyllo sheet into the tray and generously brush with oil, but do not let it pool, repeat 5 times so you have 6 oiled sheets. Place half the nut mixture on top and gently spread out. Layer another 6 filo/phyllo sheets on top, oiling each sheet generously. Spread the rest of the nut mixture on

top and finish with the last 8 sheets of filo/phyllo, brushing with oil as before. Press firmly down on the baklava so it is well compacted.

Using a very sharp knife, cut the baklava into bite-size rectangle or diamond shapes, take your time so as not to tear the pastry. Bake for 45–50 minutes until the pastry is golden brown on top. If it is beginning to burn cover with aluminium foil. The filo/phyllo pastry will curl up once baked – I love the appearance of it this way. However, some people sprinkle water onto their baklava prior to baking to prevent the fillo/phyllo from curling up, so you can do it this way if you prefer.

Immediately, while still hot, pour the cold syrup over the baklava, ensuring it seeps into every crevice. Leave to cool completely before serving. Do not cover or refrigerate as the fillo/phyllo will become soggy. When ready to serve, chop the remaining 1 tablespoon of pistachio nuts and sprinkle over the top.

This cake came together one winter evening when Mrs. B asked for a cake that we could indulge in while watching a film. I made the most of leftover ingredients at the time, but after a little subsequent tweaking, this supremely moist cake is now the most popular of all my cakes.

almond, coconut & date cake
with rose water & cardamom

For the cake:
200 g/1⅓ cups whole almonds
100 g/1⅓ cups desiccated coconut
100 g/⅔ cup stoned/pitted Medjool dates
3 eggs, beaten
150 g/¾ cup coconut palm sugar
150 ml/⅔ cup sunflower oil
50 ml/3 tablespoons coconut milk
8 cardamom pods, shells removed, seeds ground to a powder
zest of 1 unwaxed lemon, finely grated
1 teaspoon baking powder
¼ teaspoon sea salt
1 teaspoon pure vanilla extract
1 teaspoon rose water

For the syrup:
1 tablespoon coconut oil, melted
2 teaspoons freshly squeezed lemon juice
50 ml/3 tablespoons pure maple syrup

To serve:
4 tablespoons/¼ cup coconut chips, lightly roasted
2 tablespoons dried rose petals (optional)
250 ml/1 cup soya or Greek yogurt mixed with 1 tablespoon pure maple syrup and 1 teaspoon rose water

Serves 8-10

Line a 20-cm/8-inch loose-bottomed cake pan with parchment paper. Preheat the oven to 170°C (325°F) Gas 3.

Place the almonds and desiccated coconut in a food processor and blitz until the almonds are very finely chopped, but not a paste, remove to a bowl. Add the dates and eggs into the processor and blitz until the dates are finely chopped and mixed into the eggs. Add into the bowl with the almonds and the rest of the cake ingredients and mix thoroughly until well combined. Pour into the prepared cake pan and level out. Bake in the centre of the oven for 40–45 minutes or until a skewer inserted into the centre comes out clean. Remove and leave to cool for 10 minutes, then turn out of the pan onto a cooling rack.

Combine all the syrup ingredients together and drizzle half over the cake. When ready to serve, pile the coconut chips and rose petals, if using, onto the centre of the cake and drizzle over the remaining syrup. This cake is particularly nice served a little warm with the cool yogurt on the side.

Unlike pretty much any other seasonal fruit or vegetable, 'forced' and out of season rhubarb (end of December to March) is better for cooking with. Covered and deprived of light, its stems shoot upwards in search of the sun, resulting in pale pink stalks that are less fibrous then their naturally grown cousins, with a more subtle and elegant sourness.

rhubarb crumble
with maple & cinnamon ice cream

800 g/1¾ lbs. forced rhubarb, trimmed

210 g/2 cups coconut palm sugar

zest of 1 unwaxed lemon, peeled off in strips

1 teaspoon pure vanilla extract

30 g/2½ tablespoons sunflower spread (non-hydrogenated)

30 g/2 tablespoons coconut butter

80 g/⅔ cup white spelt flour

70 g/½ cup rolled oats

50 g/⅓ cup whole almonds, lightly crushed

For the ice cream:

2 cinnamon sticks, broken in half

1½ teaspoons ground cinnamon

800 ml/3⅓ cups coconut milk

100 g/½ cup coconut palm sugar

80 ml/⅓ cup maple syrup

pinch of sea salt

3 tablespoons cornflour/cornstarch

ice cream maker

Serves 6–8

For the ice cream, put half the coconut milk in a heavy-bottomed saucepan with the cinnamon (sticks and ground), coconut palm sugar, maple syrup and salt and heat through to dissolve. Place the cornflour/cornstarch in a bowl and very slowly whisk in the remaining coconut milk, 1 tablespoon at a time, until there are no lumps. Add this into the saucepan and cook over a medium-high heat, stirring constantly, until the mixture becomes noticeably thicker, about 4–5 minutes. Once thick, remove from the heat and strain through a sieve/strainer into a large bowl. Place parchment paper directly onto the surface to prevent a skin from forming and leave to cool, then refrigerate until completely chilled. You can use a freezer to speed this up.

Put the mixture into an ice cream maker and churn according to the instructions. If you don't have one, pour the mixture into a wide, flat (preferably metal) tray and place in the freezer. After 40 minutes or so, remove and use a fork to mix and break down the ice crystals. Repeat this process twice more. At the final stage, blitz in a food processor to make it really smooth. Then return to the tray and leave in the freezer to set fully. Remove 15 minutes before serving to soften.

For the crumble, preheat the oven to 200°C (400°F) Gas 6. Cut the rhubarb into 5 cm/2 inch chunks. Place a large, heavy-based pot over a medium heat. Add in the rhubarb, 150 g/¾ cup of the coconut palm sugar, the lemon peel and vanilla extract. Rhubarb is a sour fruit, and I like some of this sourness to shine through. If you don't, you can add in more sugar, but no more then about 50 g/¼ cup. Cook over a low heat for about 15 minutes until the rhubarb is tender, but not falling apart and the sugar has become a syrup. Remove from the heat and set aside. In a large bowl rub the sunflower spread and coconut butter into the flour until you have gravel-size lumps of flour. Add in the rolled oats, remaining sugar, crushed almonds and a pinch of salt and mix. Place the rhubarb in a medium pie dish, remove the lemon peel, and top with the crumble. Don't press down. Bake for about 25 minutes until golden brown.

Leave to cool for 5 minutes then serve with a scoop of ice cream.

This tart is all about the blueberries – a blueberry compote lines the tart and then a small mountain of tumbling blueberries are heaped on top. It's best served chilled on a summer's day when the fruit is in season. I have purposely not drowned the berries in a syrup that cements it all together, as I like the berries as fresh and natural as possible. It does mean it's trickier to serve as the berries tumble off, but the rustic look adds to the charm!

fresh blueberry tart

225 g/1⅔ cups white spelt flour

¼ teaspoons sea salt

120 g/generous ½ cup coconut palm sugar, plus 1 tablespoon

50 g/3 tablespoons dairy-free butter (e.g. sunflower butter – buy non-hydrogenated)

60 g/4 tablespoons vegetable fat/shortening (buy non-hydrogenated)

1 egg, beaten together with 1 teaspoon water

2 tablespoons cornflour/cornstarch

zest of 1 unwaxed lemon, finely grated, and 1 tablespoon freshly squeezed juice

900 g/2 lbs. blueberries

small handful of fresh mint leaves

1 teaspoon xylitol, ground to a fine powder

Serves 10-12

Sift the flour into a large bowl. Add in the salt, 1 tablespoon coconut palm sugar, dairy-free butter and vegetable fat/shortening and cut into small chunks with a knife. With your hands high, rub the dairy-free butter and vegetable fat/shortening into the flour until it resembles breadcrumbs. A food processor also works.

Slowly add in the egg and water mixture a tablespoon at a time, forking the mixture together as you go. Bring the dough together with your hands until it is in a smooth ball. If it is still crumbly and not coming together, add a little bit more liquid, being careful not to overdo it.

Gently flatten into a round, wrap in clingfilm/plastic wrap and place in the fridge until very cold.

Preheat the oven to 180°C (360°F) Gas 4. Once the pastry is cold, roll it out and line a 25 cm/10 inch tart pan. If you like, you can roll it between 2 sheets of clingfilm/plastic wrap to make it easier. Bake the tart blind for about 20 minutes. Remove the blind baking weights and return to the oven for a further 5–10 minutes until the base is dry and biscuity. Remove and cool on a wire rack.

Stir together the cornflour/cornstarch and lemon juice making sure there are no lumps and add to a pan with a little over ½ the blueberries, lemon zest and 120 g/generous ½ cup of coconut palm sugar. Stir over a medium-high heat for 10–15 minutes, squishing the berries as you go, until it is the consistency of a thick, soft jam. Leave to cool completely, then pour into the cold pastry case and smooth over. Tumble on the remaining blueberries, cover and refrigerate until well chilled. When ready to serve, scatter over as much mint as you like and dust with a little of the ground xylitol. Some yogurt or ice cream on the side is delicious.

Who's Josie, I hear you cry? Well that was my question too when I first tasted this delicious traditional Irish tea cake that my grandmother always has at the ready when you come over. Josie was the mother of a great friend of my grandmother's, and so good was her recipe that my grandmother has been using it for almost 60 years. I was very hesitant to tweak it, but as the only real change is using coconut palm sugar and spelt flour instead of cane sugar and white flour – they actually taste pretty much identical. 'Brack' comes from the Irish word 'brac', meaning speckled, referring to the dried fruit dotted throughout, and traditionally it is made at Halloween. A ring, or coin is often baked into the cake as a sign for the future, and of course as a child, nothing in life seemed more important then getting the slice with the lucky charm inside. My siblings and I took this as a licence to eat as much barmbrack as we could, hacking off huge slices until we found our golden treasure! The sultanas/golden raisins must be soaked overnight, so remember to start the night before.

Josie's Irish barmbrack

450 g/3 cups sultanas/ golden raisins (50 % currants another option)

350 ml/1½ cups cold Chai tea (Josie's recipe uses strong black tea, but I love the extra spice in Chai!)

225 g/1¾ cups white spelt flour

200 g/1 cup coconut palm sugar

½ teaspoon mixed spice

½ teaspoon ground cinnamon

¼ teaspoon freshly grated nutmeg

zest of 1 orange or lemon, finely grated

2 teaspoons baking powder

2 eggs, lightly beaten

salted butter or non-dairy alternative, to serve

450 g/1 lb. loaf pan, lined with parchment paper

Serves 10–12

Steep the sultanas/golden raisins in the cold tea overnight. The next day, preheat oven to 180°C (360°F) Gas 4.

In a bowl, mix together the flour, coconut palm sugar, spices, orange or lemon zest, baking powder and sultanas/golden raisins, including the cold tea. Add in the lightly beaten eggs and combine.

Pour the mixture into the prepared loaf pan and bake in the centre of the oven for about 1½ hours until a skewer comes out clean. If it looks like it is going to burn on top, cover with aluminium foil. Remove and leave to cool for 10 minutes before turning it out onto a wire rack. In Ireland, it is served in thick slices with Irish salted butter slathered on top. It is equally delicious with a non-dairy butter and a little sprinkle of sea salt. My favourite is extra virgin coconut butter – it is divine!

Granita is a lovely way to finish off a meal. Light and refreshing, it really showcases the natural flavours of whichever fruit you use. Here, beautiful winter blood orange and persimmon (see buying tips below), make for a perfect partnership and a really refreshing dessert.

winter granita of blood orange & persimmon

2 very ripe 'hachiya' persimmons (flesh should be completely soft, almost falling apart)
juice of 8 blood oranges (about 550 ml/2¼ cups)
zest of 1 unwaxed lemon
6 tablespoons pure maple syrup
pinch of sea salt

Serves 4–6

Cut the persimmons in half and scoop out their gelatinous, almost liquid flesh. Place in a food processor with the blood orange juice, lemon zest, maple syrup and salt. Blitz on and off until the persimmon flesh is puréed and everything is well combined. Transfer the liquid to a shallow tray, preferably metal, and carefully place it in the freezer. After 1 hour, using a fork, drag the ice crystals away from the edges. Do not whisk it all up as you would with a sorbet, as you want to keep the large crystals of ice intact. Place it back in the freezer for a further 2 hours to set properly. When ready to serve, remove from the freezer and scrape with a fork until rough; this will take a bit of effort, as the granita will be fully set. Spoon into chilled glasses and serve.

PERSIMMON TIPS: Persimmon (also known as Sharon fruit and cachi) have two varieties, hachiya and fuyu.

They look quite similar, but have completely different textures and uses. Confusingly, the hachiya and fuyu varieties will often be sold under one general name, either persimmon, Sharon fruit or cachi, but really it is their specific name that is most important, so be sure to ask if you are unsure. Round and larger than fuyu, hachiya is astringent, extremely tart and very firm when unripe, so don't attempt to eat them then. During ripening, they will go from orange to a very deep orange, almost red colour, and their flesh will become completely soft, almost exploding out from their skin, and gelatinous once opened.

Fuyu are smaller and squatter in shape, and are often sold in the UK as Sharon fruit. They remain quite firm on the outside, with a slightly softer, yet still slightly crunchy inside. With a mild sweetness, they are ideal for eating as you would an apple.

One of the things I adore about London are the great food markets. There you can sample a whole range of interesting ingredients and dishes, cooked by people who are passionate about one specific area, so they really know their stuff, whether it be lobster rolls, vegan cakes or Chinese pork buns. Last summer at Maltby street market I tasted some stunning ice cream, flavoured with really unusual ingredients. The basil and lemon was my favourite though, the sweet perfume of the basil leaves perfectly matched with the sharper citrus juice and zest. Here, I've used coconut milk as the base – it works really well and noone guesses it's dairy-free!

basil & lemon ice cream

800 ml/3⅓ cups coconut milk
55 g/¼ cup xylitol
90 ml/⅓ cup pure maple syrup
50 large basil leaves, roughly torn, plus a few baby leaves to serve
2 unwaxed lemons, zest peeled off in strips and 2 tablespoons freshly squeezed juice
pinch of sea salt
3 tablespoons cornflour/cornstarch

ice cream maker (optional)

Serves 6–8

Pour ½ the coconut milk into a heavy-based saucepan with the xylitol, maple syrup, basil leaves, lemon peel and salt and heat through to dissolve the sugar. Place the cornflour/cornstarch in a separate bowl and very slowly whisk in the remaining coconut milk, 1 tablespoon at a time, making sure there are no lumps. Stir this into the saucepan over a medium-high heat until the mixture begins to bubble gently. Cook like this for a few minutes stirring all the time until it becomes noticeably thicker. To test, coat the back of a wooden spoon and run your finger through it – if the line holds and does not drip, it is ready.

Turn off the heat and leave for 20 minutes stirring now and again, then strain through a sieve/strainer into a bowl, squeezing the basil and lemon peel to extract flavour. Add in the lemon juice and combine.

Place parchment paper directly onto the surface of the mixture to prevent a skin from forming and leave to cool, then refrigerate until completely chilled. You can use a freezer to speed this up. Once chilled, freeze in an ice cream maker or if you don't have one, pour the mixture into a wide flat (preferably metal) tray and place in the freezer. After 40 minutes or so, remove and use a fork to mix and break down the ice crystals. Repeat this process twice more.

At the final stage, blitz in a food processor to make it really smooth. Then return to the tray and leave in the freezer to set fully. Remove 15 minutes before serving to soften. Serve with a few baby basil leaves scattered over.

I had a client who decided he wanted to stop eating dairy for health reasons and was lamenting all the dishes he would no longer eat, rice pudding being the greatest loss. He was quite insistent that none of my non-dairy tricks would compare to his preferred method of using full-fat milk to cook the rice and then adding in double cream at the end, so it seemed as though it might be a lost cause. Not wanting to admit defeat, I tried out a few options and eventually won him over with this luscious and thick pudding made using coconut milk and cream, and rice milk. For the toppings, feel free to use whatever you like. Medjool dates and nut butter swirled though the pudding is another favourite.

coconut rice pudding
with blueberries & maple syrup

150 g/³⁄₄ cup risotto rice, carnaroli or arborio

400-ml/14-fl. oz. can coconut milk

600 ml/2½ cups rice or almond milk

1 teaspoon pure vanilla extract

½ teaspoon ground cinnamon

good pinch of grated nutmeg, about ¼ teaspoon

pinch of sea salt

3 tablespoons pure maple syrup, plus extra to drizzle over

handful of frozen blueberries

Serves 4

Rinse the rice thoroughly under running water and add to a pot with the coconut milk and rice milk and bring to a boil. Reduce the heat to low and simmer gently for about 20–35 minutes, stirring regularly to ensure the rice does not stick to the bottom. By this stage the rice should be cooked through with a thick and creamy consistency. Stir in the vanilla extract, cinnamon, nutmeg, salt and maple syrup and taste, adding a little more of anything you particularly like.

When ready to serve, ladle the hot rice into bowls and add in a few frozen blueberries (or whatever topping you choose), straight from the freezer. Drizzle over a little maple syrup and serve immediately. The blueberries will thaw out in the hot pudding, leaving gorgeous inky pools of juice as you eat.

Posset, a very English dessert, is like a very rich and creamy lemon mousse, and a little goes a long way. Quince, which look a little like large misshapen pears, have a very firm perfumed flesh that benefits from cooking, drawing out their wonderful flavour. If quince are not in season, you can always substitute them with fresh raspberries or blackberries, which make another lovely accompaniment.

lemon posset with roast quince

450 ml/2 cups soya cream/soy creamer

100 g/½ cup xylitol

1½ teaspoons agar flakes

zest of 1 unwaxed lemon, finely grated, and 100 ml/scant ½ cup freshly squeezed lemon juice (roughly 2 lemons)

2 quince

100 g scant/½ cup pure maple syrup

peel of 1 orange

1 vanilla pod/bean, split in half lengthways

50 ml/3 tablespoons water

Serves 4

Place the soya cream/soy creamer, xylitol and agar flakes in a pan and bring to a boil, reduce the heat to a simmer and cook for 8 minutes stirring now and again until the agar flakes have completely dissolved. Remove from the heat, add in the lemon juice and most of the zest and stir to combine. Leave to infuse for 10 minutes then strain through a fine sieve/strainer into a jug/small pitcher. Pour into 4 small glasses or little espresso cups and refrigerate for at least 3 hours until very well chilled and set.

Preheat the oven to 170°C (340°F) Gas 3. Rinse the quince under running water and rub off the fine coating of fluffy hair. Cut the quince into wedges, roughly 8 for each one. Place on a baking sheet and toss with the maple syrup, orange peel, vanilla pod/bean and water, ensuring everything is well combined. Cover with aluminium foil and bake for 1 hour. Remove the foil, stir the quince and continue to cook for 30 minutes until they are a deep pinky orange colour.

Once set, remove the lemon posset from the fridge and add a little of the remaining lemon zest to the top of each one. Serve on a plate with a few wedges of quince alongside.

The chocolate tart from my first book 'The Guilt-Free Gourmet' has been insanely popular, so I thought this mousse would appeal, as it is even easier to whip up. For the uninitiated, yes, that is an avocado in the ingredients list, but don't knock it until you've tried it! It has just as much chocolatey goodness going on as the most dairy-laden mousse out there. The rosemary caramel is deep and rich in flavour from the coconut palm sugar and so good you could eat it by the spoon. While I'm not suggesting it counts as one of your 5 a day, it's certainly better then the average refined cane sugar caramel!

chocolate mousse
with rosemary caramel & raspberries

3 tablespoons coconut oil

2 large ripe avocados

4 tablespoons/¼ cup unsweetened cocoa powder

4 tablespoons/¼ cup pure maple syrup

1 teaspoons/¼ cup pure vanilla extract

sea salt

100 g/½ cup coconut palm sugar

200 ml/¾ cup coconut milk

2 stalks/sprigs rosemary, plus a few leaves to serve

about 15 raspberries

Serves 4

Melt the coconut oil in a heat-proof bowl over a saucepan of simmering water.

Add the flesh of the avocados, cocoa powder, maple syrup, vanilla and a good pinch of sea salt to a food processor and blitz for a few seconds. Add in the melted coconut oil and blitz until completely smooth. Remove to a bowl, cover and refrigerate for at least 2 hours.

To make the caramel, place the coconut milk and coconut palm sugar in a saucepan over a medium-high heat. Bring to a boil stirring all the time, then reduce the heat, add the rosemary and a pinch of sea salt, and simmer for 10 minutes, stirring on and off, until you have a thick, viscous caramel.

When ready to serve, warm the caramel, and then spoon the set chocolate mousse in a misshapen mound onto the centre of a cold bowl or plate. Drizzle over the warm rosemary caramel, add a few raspberries onto each dish and scatter over some rosemary leaves and a very small pinch of sea salt. Serve immediately.

Index

Acknowledgements

Making a cookbook look this beautiful ain't easy! There are so many minds and hands that slave away behind the scenes and I feel so privileged to have been able to work with such a wonderful group of people – my recipes would be nothing without them. Thanks to Cindy and Julia for believing in me in the first place, you have been a joy to work with once again. Nathan, for your way with words and for teasing my mass of text into shape. Leslie for your great accent that makes me feel like I am in a cool American TV drama about cookbook publishing and, of course, your very keen eye! Maria for designing so beautifully, Megan, the best art director an author could wish for and for being such fun on the shoots! Lauren, for being the nicest person on the planet, and getting my books seen by the world. Tara, you are a hoot to work with and I love your photos – you have brought my food to life, thank you, and also to your lovely family and assistant Sue. Jo, your props are so stunning, I felt depressed every time I got home from the shoot! To Fiona, Livia and Rhian for your invaluable assistance in the kitchen.

And to Claudia, my witty, articulate and razor-sharp agent, thank you for everything.

To my wife and chief recipe tester Jina – you are just amazing. I could go on, but I would make everyone ill. And to the rest of my family for your brutal honesty, love and support.